ALIEN *of* EXTRAORDINARY ABILITY

eleven short plays by

Zhu Yi

For foreigners

CONTENTS

ACKNOWLEDGMENTS

Edited by
Kim Davies

Cover designed by
4aTEAM (www.4ateam.com)

Cover image created by
Zhu Liang 朱亮

PREFACE

If you are in show business, you might hear "you were extraordinary," or "that was extraordinary," from time to time. No peer would be stingy with a compliment or two while giving you a hug after a show. But, in the meantime, our less diplomatic side sets a personal higher bar for that word, "extraordinary." To my own standard, I'm not extraordinary, or important, or anything close to a big deal.

In watching and writing for theater every day, I'm learning about the infinite complexity of the world and the insignificance of myself. And after facing such continuous wonderment, no ego could last long or remain complacent. As a little fart traveling across time and space, I pursue theatre as a quixotic endeavor to make sense of life. It's where I dream, where I shit, where I experiment and fail, and experiment more. And there is no better place to do so than New York City.

I could no longer afford such a work ethic, however, once my student visa expired.

"Alien of extraordinary ability" is an alien classification used by the United States Citizenship and Immigration Services. The United States may grant a non-immigrant visa to an alien who is able to demonstrate "extraordinary ability in the sciences, arts, education, business, or athletics." "Extraordinary ability" in the arts means "a level of expertise and recognition that shows a high level of achievement." The visa is known colloquially as a "genius visa," or "artists' visa."

I started pursuing this visa in 2013, and spent months after months gathering posters, programs, reviews, interviews, publications, contracts, award certificates, and endorsements from collaborators, critics, employers, clients, and patrons... anything on a letter-size piece of paper that could suggest my talent and achievements. As artists in 21st-century America, none of us are strangers to self-promotion, grant writing, open submissions, project proposals, artistic statements, etc. However, demonstrating extraordinariness to meet the requirements of an O-1 visa is an entirely different game. To give you a glimpse:

To prove you are extraordinary, you need at least eight letters of support from people who are extraordinary in their field of expertise. To prove those people are extraordinary, you may, for example, enclose reliable press clips to show your endorsers' accomplishments. To prove those press clips are reliable, you need to find the circulation statistics of each press. But then you need to prove the authority of those statistics. A favorably reviewed or award-winning professional production may be denied as a valid credit if you wrote the play while attending school; selection for an Obie-winning playwrights' group may not be a proof of your talent if you can't provide an evidence of you "performing a critical role for the organization"; an established theatre professional who has followed your work for many years may not be eligible to testify for your talent if the very first work of yours he or she saw was an academic production...

Soon, playwriting became a luxury. My time was consumed by collecting evidence for evidence for evidence.

And my English vocabulary grew. There are so many ways to say "extraordinary" without using the word "extraordinary": remarkable, excellent, with unparalleled success, exceptionally talented, acclaimed, outstanding, brilliant, significant, distinguished, incredibly prolific, innately creative, unique, accomplished, highly appreciated, inimitable, singular, huge popularity, once-in-a-generation-talent, one of the most exciting voices… These were the words people used to describe me in their letters of support. Yet you will find these words in letters of support for every artist's visa application. This is the style strongly recommended by immigration lawyers and those who are experienced with artist visa applications. Due to the high volume of workload in the immigration office, one of the most efficient ways to stand out is to repeat the highest-level words as often as possible. But when every applicant does that, you look like a loser in comparison if you don't use the same trick.

So why do playwriting in New York City?

I'm from a country where certain individuals tend to speak for the people, and "the people" always speak for the individuals. Any voice that doesn't echo in unison with the others is edited or wiped out. However, as I grew older and traveled further, I realized this kind of violation can happen anywhere as long as people are influenced by authority, class and social strata, capital, the media, etc. When I chose playwriting as my career, it was because theatre is one of the few things that can defend our dignity as individuals, no matter who we are or what we're facing.

It's true that making theatre in New York City is extremely competitive, expensive, and unprofitable, but after battling with censorship and plagiarism in China, I find it amazing how New York allows me to focus on theatre above all else. And through years of observing and making theatre in New York, I've realized what I can contribute to the community is as much as what I need from it. The curiosity and anxiety coming from my identity as an outsider keep me on my toes and inspire me to restlessly explore the issues that the insiders ignore. And, in the meantime, as an insider in another culture, witnessing the endless hot sales of pandas, kung fu flicks, factory girls and Mao's Red Book in art and entertainment markets in America, I've never felt so strongly about my responsibility and power as a storyteller. I'm writing and will only write plays that can broaden imaginations, sweep away generalizations, and punch holes into walls built of stereotypes. I've become an unstoppable little fireball.

So far, this "fireball" has burned more than ten thousand dollars in the visa application process, including the fees to the attorneys, the translators, the immigration office, and the union. The USCIS website says the average processing time for an artist visa is two weeks, but it's been almost four months since I submitted my application. I could pay an extra $1,225 for the "premium processing service," which guarantees a response within fifteen days. However, that's not recommended by many lawyers because "sometimes it might backfire and push the immigration office to adjudicate a pending case."

I can't help but feel like I've joined a religion: sending out a prayer, but without knowing when and how God might answer; trying to be good but wondering what "good" means; devoting time and money in the hope of gaining recognition and acceptance... (Or maybe God does move in the same mysterious ways as the US visa system. Does he have angels reviewing petitions submitted by priests? Does his office ever make mistakes? How long is his waiting line? Are we being evaluated as people, or as piles of letter-size papers? Which possibility makes you more nervous?)

I have to stay in the US during the preparation and processing; if I left it's unclear when I would be allowed back. During the endless wait, I missed five productions of my plays in China, two Chinese New Year celebrations, and my father's sixtieth birthday. But what hit me the hardest was my grandma's death, which my parents hid from me for months because they wanted to protect me, not only from the pain of losing someone I loved, but also the pain of resenting myself for being absent.

In the past six years I've lived in New York, I've seen people whose work I most admired be denied for this visa, and, hence, forcefully removed from the New York theater landscape; I've seen people who hardly had professional credits receive their approvals; I've seen what bad immigration lawyers can do to people; I've seen people suffering from fraud while others benefit from forgery; I've seen people at last celebrating receiving their artist visas, and then struggling with their renewals every three years. "It's like having a clock ticking day and night inside you," they say.

I believe all the visa policies were created in the best intentions. And I believe the immigration officers are using their best judgements every day to handpick the top talent for America. However, that's just what causes the problem. As a state institution, the immigration office rates artists as if it were a professional talent agency. But even real talent agencies don't have complete accuracy in predicting their artists' careers. If you look into established artists' professional histories, you won't find many common patterns. At least when talent agencies misjudge an artist, they don't have the power to kill that artist's career. They are not authorized to forcefully remove an artist from the entire American arts and entertainment industry, but the immigration office is. "If you are gold, you will shine," the saying goes. But that doesn't mean you will shine for the one immigration officer reading your application.

Even once artists have been awarded visas, the law sets further obstacles to their careers by imposing limits on their incomes. Holders of artist visas are forbidden from working outside of the purview of their visas: for example, a writer can only receive income from writing. Whoever passed that law clearly never worked a day in theater in America. I don't know how many theater artists you know who entirely live on their theater gigs, but I haven't met many. I know a Broadway playwright who bartends, a Drama Desk Award nominee who waits tables, a Playwrights of New York Fellowship winner who tutors mathematics... It's not that they are not extraordinary enough, but that the theater industry in America is just not that profitable compared to other industries, and theater artists are rarely paid on a long-term, steady basis. A law like this puts international artists in a very vulnerable position, forcing them to choose between living in poverty and working illegally, neither of which benefits anyone. Oh, they do have a third option: leave.

An artist visa is not a mercy or an award. It doesn't guarantee a job, either, because artists must still stand up to the scrutiny of the audience, the critics, the market, and time. International playwrights don't steal jobs from American playwrights, because the plays we create are all so different. Having international artists working in American theater gives new energy to all. I'm not suggesting there should be a visa for everyone, but, from what I've witnessed and experienced, I don't find that the current artist visa policies are helping the American theater.

For now, I'm merely an alien, one of the hundreds of millions in the US. Tomorrow I may become an alien of extraordinary ability, or I may not, and I will have to leave within thirty days. Either way, I believe it's time to reexamine the artist visa policies and make a change. The purpose of such a visa is to encourage great art, and great art is less likely to happen when the artists are worn out by the demands of the system.

This book is a selection of short plays of mine written and performed between 2008 and 2015 in the US. It's a record of my collaborations with some of the most talented, daring, and devoted artists in the world. It's a portrait of who I used to be, who I aspired to be, and who I might be in the future. It is not more supporting material for my "extraordinariness," but I do hope that you can see my humble, ever-onward pursuit of that word, as I believe an artist thrives in the reaching, not the arriving.

Zhu Yi
April 28, 2015
New York City

WEDDING

WEDDING was performed at Schapiro Theatre in New York City, January 29-31, 2009, as part of "Hello, Stranger," a short play showcase. It was directed by Marios Theocharous, produced by Camila Le-Bert and Erin Moughon, and stage managed by Pisa Waikwamdee. The cast was as follows:

WEDDING GUEST	Jason Goedken
WEDDING GUEST	Nate Grams
WEDDING GUEST	Caitlin Johnston
WEDDING GUEST	Whitney Morse

Performance Notes

Although there are thirty different roles, the play allows for flexible casting of any number of actors.

A wedding ceremony in early afternoon.

GUEST 1

At the end of the summer, finally the heat fades out.

It has been drizzling for weeks. We sit inside, listen to the rain hitting the roof and people's loud greetings to each other.

Sister's aunt, aunt's father, father's mother, mother's son, son's cousin, cousin's sister-in-law, brother-in-law, mother-in-law, father-in-law, grandma-in-law, grandpa-in-law… Two big families mix together. But you can distinguish them easily by their appearance features — like the products from two brands. No matter how hard you've been washed, bleached, or dyed, the logos are still all over your body. Magnificent and boring.

The bride's mother is holding a Louis Vuitton bag. Yes, just like that.

GUEST 2 (MALE)

The banquet hasn't started. I am staring at the red chopsticks and the silver spoon on the table, imagining how they'd feel. Cold and solid. That turns me on.

The girl sitting next to me keeps staring at the smoked salmon. They arrange my seat next to hers. Which means she is single and of the right age for me.

GUEST 3 (FEMALE)

He looks so short in his white suit. She looks hardly beautiful. The handmade dress doesn't help. I heard they met in a bar.

He caught her caught him caught a glimpse of her — He bought her a drink — She laughed properly when he told a dry joke — He asked for her number — First date — Second date — Would you like to come upstairs for a coffee? — Valentine's — Birthday — Anniversary — Meet the parents — And... Bang!

We are here.

What I am saying is: she could be anyone. Last night I was in a bar. A man offered to buy me a drink. Then he told a dry joke. I laughed politely. But when he asked for my number, I didn't give it to him. He was too short. Wow. Does that mean I may have rejected my future husband?

It's very possible that I rejected this groom once somewhere for the same reason, but I can't recall now, neither can he of course. But imagine if I didn't. One thing for sure: The handmade dress would look worthy on me.

GUEST 4

The speech is too long. I am hungry.

GUEST 5 (FEMALE)

Every time I watch a bride's father walking his daughter down the aisle. I cry. Doesn't matter whether it's a movie or a real wedding.

I am that kind of person who could easily be moved. The national flag, orphans, Princess Diana, Titanic, sometimes even Mr. Bean. They call it "Low Melting Point."

My son always laughs at me. He says the last thing he wants to see is me crying at his wedding. I always wonder if that's the reason he turned to be gay.

Since then I attend more weddings. And I cry more emotionally than ever. And I feel...I feel... *(Whispers)* not bad!

GUEST 4

The speech is too long. I am hungry.

4

GUEST 6 (MALE)

When the gift list was passed to me, all the items had already been marked, except one, the most expensive one—a rosewood table. Fuck! Why should I pay $1000 for someone's wedding, when my own wife is divorcing me?

I don't know how much luck a fucking rosewood table can bring to your marriage. I don't know. When we got married, no one gave us anything like that. All we had was vodka and rock music. We were dancing and drinking with our best friends all night long. And in the end, everyone was dead drunk. The two of us passed out on the wedding bed, snoring. Didn't even take off clothes. The next morning when we woke up and saw each other. It felt like... uh... like... more vodka and rock music!

Now, seven years passed, she wants to marry another guy. Will they host a wedding in a garden like this? Will anyone buy them a rosewood table? Great! I should buy them a fucking rosewood table of top quality! Every day you sit at it and eat and remember how we woke up on that first morning!!

PRIEST

Now you may kiss the bride.

> *The ceremony finishes. Reception starts. Late afternoon.*

GUEST 7 (MALE)

Have we met before? I don't think so. If we did, I would definitely remember such a lovely lady like you. May I have the honor? *(They start to dance)* Yeah, I am the bride's brother. We grew up together. Such a sweetheart, isn't she? Everyone adores her. John is a lucky man. They are just... perfect together! Don't you agree? So, are you a sister or cousin of his? ...Oh! You are his ex-girlfriend! No, no, nothing. Just a little surprised. (Oh god.) Are you ok? Good? Good! Life goes on. That's a good thing. She never

5

met you, did she? That's another good thing. Good… Good. I am thirsty. Can I get you anything? No? Ok, I am just going to get some… I'll be right back.

GUEST 8 (FEMALE)

Kim! Don't waste food! If you stay naughty I won't bring you next time. Sit down! Why can't you behave yourself like that girl at the next table? See? She is four years old too. Put down the bread! You are embarrassing me!

Well! I don't want you! Mama likes good kids. Mama will take that girl home!

Okay okay don't cry! Mama loves you! Don't cry! Mama will take Kim home. Look there, look there! Isn't the bride beautiful? Kim baby, good girl, don't cry. Don't cry! Don't cry so loud. Don't, please…

DOOOOOOON'T CRY! SHUT UP!

GUEST 9

Salmon is good.

GUEST 10

Salmon is good.

GUEST 11

Salmon is good.

GUEST 12

Salmon is good.

GUEST 13

CHEERS! For health, peace, and love!

GUEST 14 (FEMALE)

Dad is drunk. You shouldn't let him drink. Did you bring his pills? I can't believe it! When mom was alive, she always knew how to take the best care of him. I am not blaming you. All I try to say is, being a wife means more than being young and pretty.

By the way, I don't think dad enjoys sitting in his wheelchair and watching you endlessly dancing with boys.

GUEST 15 (MALE)

He is hot, isn't he? He is smiling at me! Should I go buy him a drink? Oh, you are right. It's a wedding. Drinks are free. Shit.

Wedding.

Weeeeee-ddinnnnng.

That word tickles me, stirs in me. Gives me an itch to something, some... some... great thing. I don't know. Ok, I'm going to try my luck. Nothing could go wrong. After all, we are at a wedding, aren't we?

GUEST 16 (MALE)

I don't recognize everyone in my family. I guess some of them only show up at weddings and funerals. So I have to be careful when I hook up. No one wants to French-kiss an aunt or niece.

GUEST 17 (FEMALE)

Every time the bride is about to toss the bouquet, everyone gathers around her, fighting to be the closest one. But I know that's a mistake. My Ph.D. degree wasn't for nothing. The bouquet never lands in the front row. People sometimes notice that, but they are too excited to give it more thought. Most girls know nothing about dynamics. They think dynamics are irrelevant to marriage, but they will regret their ignorance when I get the bouquet. And the next time the bride tosses the bouquet, they will again stand in the front line! Argh. What can I say? Some people just deserve to be single.

GUEST 18

3 – 2 – 1 – Cheeeeeeese!

3 – 2 – 1 – Cheeeeeeese! Sorry I blinked.

One more please! 3 – 2 – 1 – Cheeeeeeese!

Hmm... I like it. *(Pause)* Actually, do you mind... Thank you!

3 – 2 – 1 – Cheeeeeeese!

Great! Remember to send it to me!

Can we do one more? ...3 – 2 – 1 – Cheeeeeeese!

GUEST 19

Wish you live to old age in conjugal bliss! Wish you all the best!

GUEST 20

Let's dance! Ladies and gentlemen, boys and girls! Dance!!

GUEST 21 (MALE)

I couldn't stop thinking about you since last time we met at the funeral.

GUEST 22 (MALE)

Me neither.

> *Time has passed. Lights change. Sun has set, but not entirely dark yet.*

GUEST 23 (MALE)

Please listen to the rain dripping on the roof. So quiet. So lazy.

Our little angel just became a man's wife. Isn't it beautiful? And soon we're going to have a little little angel. And another one, and two, and three… You are going to read the fairy tales to our grandsons and granddaughters, but playing chess with me will surely be more fun for them. They all come to me and ask me to teach them. After they have learned, I can still beat them easily, but I pretend to lose sometimes, so that they will always enjoy playing with their grandpa.

Don't worry. When I play with the kids, you will surprise them with the magical hot chocolate you make. Oh how much they love their grandma and her hot chocolate. And that even makes me jealous a little.

And when, one day, chess and hot chocolate can no longer keep those kids, we'll start to get busy again with attending their weddings one after another.

Isn't it beautiful?

It's the best miracle in the world.

GUEST 24 (FEMALE)

Has the rain stopped? I didn't bring my umbrella. It wasn't so bad when I left home… I don't know. Maybe I will do some laundry when I get home. My sheets haven't been changed for two months. I simply didn't have the time. I wrote until 3:00 AM last night. My editor is a dog, no, a wolf running after me all the time.

Oh, really? The one on the corner is cheaper? Good to know! The one I always go to keeps raising prices. It was $2.15 per load when I first moved here, now is $2.75.

No, I can't go now. It would ruin my shoes. Those are my best shoes. I wrote thirty thousand words and bought them. Oh, thanks. Yeah, I am proud. Yep, that's what I'm trying to be. Thank you for saying that. *(Pause)* So I am not leaving now. I have no idea how long I would have to wait. I know it's been raining for weeks. I just don't want to ruin my shoes.

GUEST 25 (MALE)

Can I give you a ride, miss? It's still early. We can have some coffee if you like.

GUEST 26 (FEMALE)

The cake looks really good. Did you get a piece? Me too, but you see, everyone is leaving now. No one cares about the cake. Maybe I can find a box to take it home. You know, after we leave, they will just throw it away, so why don't we take it? It would be perfect for breakfast. Would you please pass me the plate there? Yes, that one. My daughter loves cake, especially this vanilla flavor, but I have to be quick. She hates me doing this. I don't remember since when, whatever I do, my daughter will always give me this look… I thought I should be the one educating her, but since when our roles have switched. Last time, she said to me, "You are embarrassing me." Oh! Listen to that! Embarrassing her? For what? I am not stealing. I am a guest just like you, right? The banquet was prepared for us. Young people always exaggerate things.

Anyway, if I don't tell her where this cake is from, she will be so happy eating it, after all it's such a good cake! Don't you agree? That plate please. Thanks! You know, it's not about money. I just don't like wasting food. But anyway, you may have noticed, cakes are terribly expensive these days! I know the price. My daughter loves cakes, so I know the price.

Could you please pass me that bowl of apples? My daughter also loves apples.

GUEST 27

3 – 2 – 1 – CHEEEEEEEEESE!

GUEST 28

He broke his leg in the last dance. Poor man. His wife just keeps blaming him for drinking too much, but she herself looks even drunker than him.

Poor man. It was already the last dance, at the end of the summer. Poor man!

GUEST 29 (FEMALE)

Have you seen my daughter? Have you seen my daughter? I can't find her anywhere. God! If the newlyweds take one look at my daughter, they would never consider having a child.

Kim! Come out! Kim! Come out…! Mama doesn't have time and PATIENCE!

GUEST 30 (FEMALE, CHILD)

When we get married, can we invite as many guests as they did?

Can we have many bottles of champagne as well?

Can I have a handmade wedding dress?

Can you be not so short?

Can I play with your toy car for a while?

I love you!

End of play.

DEEP BLUE

DEEP BLUE was performed at Schapiro Theatre in New York City in March 2009 as part of Collaboration Class at Columbia University Theatre Arts, under the mentorship of Anne Bogart. The theme of the assignment was "Current Event." The play was directed by Jonathan Vandenberg and the dramaturgy was by Molly Mullen. The cast was as follows:

GARRY KASPAROV	Grayson Powell
GARRY KASPAROV'S MOTHER, MASHA, and POLINA	Whitney Morse
SOMEONE	Molly Mullen

Performance Notes

The play was inspired by a pair of famous six-game human-computer chess matches played between the IBM supercomputer Deep Blue and the World Chess Champion Garry Kasparov.

The roles of Garry Kasparov's mother, his first wife Masha, and his daughter Polina can be played by one actor. At the end of the play, I suggest the actors not take a curtain call or reveal themselves. Only the laptops should take the curtain call, with the help of the actors.

Description of Characters

Garry Kasparov: Grandmaster chess player, male, Russian, forty years old

Garry Kasparov's mother: In her thirties

Masha: Garry Kasparov's girlfriend and first wife, in her thirties

Polina: Garry Kasparov's daughter, eight years old

Someone: No identity; in black

Lights up on one side of the stage. GARRY and a laptop sit at a cocktail table, facing each other. The chairs are exquisite. A chess board on the table. GARRY ponders.

GARRY
(To the laptop)

Do you mind if I ask for a glass of water? Do you want one too? …Oh! Of course you don't! Sorry, I forgot. You are a machine! What would they call that? …Yes! "Short circuit."

GARRY raises his empty glass. SOMEONE comes to the table with a bottle. She pours water into Garry's glass.

GARRY

Ice please.

SOMEONE adds some ice cubes into his glass.

GARRY

Careful. Careful. Do not splash a single drop on that gentleman. It might kill him.

SOMEONE leaves.
GARRY drinks his water.

GARRY

You may wonder why I come back again and again. I've won, twice. I've lost, once. The last time was a draw. The government and the media were freaking out—"Our best chess player is beaten by a machine! We are going to be enslaved by the robots!" Are you kidding me?

Sometimes I feel the chess match between you and me is just like a finger-guessing game between my left hand and right hand. Don't get me wrong. I am not saying we are brothers. You should know, we human beings use a part of our brain to learn chess, and another part to create you. To be frank, this match is only an entertainment between two parts of my brain. So don't take it too seriously. Mr.… Blue. May I call you Deep? I guess it's your first name.

Well, Deep, even if you win this time, it would be humans' victory. Plus, you won't.

GARRY moves a knight.

GARRY

Check.
Your turn, Deep.

Lights up on the other side of the stage. A woman, GARRY'S MOTHER, lying on the ground. She is in the middle of giving birth.

GARRY

Mother?

GARRY'S MOTHER doesn't see GARRY. She is struggling and screaming.

GARRY'S MOTHER
AAAAH! Push! AH! PUSH! JESUS CHRIST! Come out!

GARRY
Mother! Are you ok? What's going on? Are you sick? Somebody help!

GARRY wants to walk to her, but somehow he cannot stand up from the chair. And GARRY'S MOTHER doesn't hear him.

GARRY'S MOTHER
AAAH! COME OOOOOOONN!

She has made it. A baby, no, a laptop, pops out from under her skirt. And we hear the signature Windows start-up sound.

She is exhausted, but she picks up the laptop and holds it in her arms with love.

GARRY'S MOTHER
Oh, it's a boy! Look at you… How beautiful you are! Look at these blue eyes. Your hair is as black as your father's.

GARRY
Are you ok, Mom? Who brought you here? What are you doing?

GARRY'S MOTHER kisses the laptop.

GARRY'S MOTHER
Let's find a name for you.

She thinks.

GARRY'S MOTHER
Garry. Yes! Garry! Do you like this name?

GARRY
Mom! *I* am Garry! I am here!

But suddenly he realizes something. He turns to that laptop sitting across the table.

17

GARRY

What the hell did you do?

> *GARRY'S MOTHER hums a lullaby to the laptop.*
>
> *A projected computer screen lights up somewhere on stage. A music player window pops up on the screen. It repeats the same lullaby.*

GARRY'S MOTHER

What a genius baby!

> *The music player plays another sound cue. It's a baby voice saying "Mama! Mama!" GARRY'S MOTHER is touched.*

GARRY'S MOTHER

OH, MY DEAR! Say it again!

> *"Mama! Mama!"*
> *GARRY'S MOTHER bursts into tears and kisses the laptop.*

GARRY'S MOTHER

Yes, my son! Yes!

> *Lights down on GARRY'S MOTHER's side of the stage.*
>
> *GARRY stares into the darkness, feeling unease. 'Am I daydreaming?' he wonders.*

The laptop has finished its move. It's Garry's turn. GARRY forces his attention back to the chess board. He ponders.

GARRY

You know what? I can defeat you with a simple little move—remove your battery. Have you thought about that? But I won't. I will never do that!—because I am MAN. That's the <u>nobility</u> of MAN, which you would never understand. I know you've studied every single piece of information about me. Yeah, I was born in Baku. Of course, of course, you've memorized all the names of my family members. You analyzed my reaction mode based on hundreds of matches they stored on your chips. You even did a research on how indoor temperature changes affect my strategizing. Bravo! You're going to beat me—so you think.

But there is something you could never experience in your limited mechanical life and some areas you could never access by calculating. And that's where I come from and how I'm going to beat you.

He moves a castle.

GARRY

Check again. Watch out, Deep.

Lights up on the other side of the stage.

In a bar.

A laptop sits at the bar counter. SOMEONE stands behind the counter as bartender. She asks the laptop something, and then puts a glass in front of the laptop, fills it with water and adds some ice cubes. MASHA enters the bar and sits next to the laptop.

19

GARRY

Masha? What are you doing here?

MASHA can't hear him. Laptop "says"
something to MASHA.

MASHA
(To laptop)

You talking to me…? Oh, thanks. *(Touches her necklace)* It's a gift
from my grandma. My name is Masha… Hi Garry. *(She shakes its*
"hand") …Yeah… I am by myself. But no, thank you. I am not that
kind of girl. We hardly know each other, yet.

GARRY

It was the first time we met…

A window of a PDF file or a Word file pops up
on the projected computer screen. It's an
extremely detailed profile of Garry Kasparov,
including date of birth, nationality, education
background, working experience, awards,
hobbies, height and weight, allergies, favorite
food, favorite football team…

MASHA
(Reading the profile)

That's very sincere of you… Oh my god! You are Garry
Kasparov?! THE Garry Kasparov?! Are you serious? I can't believe
it! I am talking to Garry Kasparov!

As MASHA types on the laptop, an online
chatting window pops up on the projection
screen:

"Masha says: I'm ur huge fan, Mr.Kasparov!
(Smiley face icon.)

20

Garry says: Plz call me Garry. (Cool guy with sunglasses icon.)

Masha says: I'd never imagine a grandmaster like u go 2 bars like us."

Pause.

"Garry says: I keep thinking abt u since last night. (Heart icon.)
Masha says: Me 2! (Shy face icon.)
Garry says: (Rose icon.)"

Online chatting ends.

Masha and the laptop sit side by side, "holding hands." They "kiss."

It rains. MASHA runs into the house holding the laptop. She wipes the rain from her face and its face… They sit on the bed… they lie down… They start to make love. A webpage pops up on the projected computer screen. It plays a porn movie. MASHA lies on the bed and holds the laptop with passion.

GARRY

Stop! Stop that! Masha!

GARRY wants to get to her, but he can't move. He shouts at the laptop across the chessboard.

GARRY

What have you done to my wife? What do you want?

21

MASHA

Oh... Yes! Yes! Oh! Oh! Ah... Deep! Deep! Deep!

GARRY looks at them with fear.

GARRY

(To his opponent the laptop)

Is she calling you? IS SHE CALLING YOUR NAME?! Stop that! Stop!! Stop!!

Lights down on MASHA's part of the stage.

GARRY

What was that?! Tell me! What did you do to her! ...That was ridiculous! I swear to God if you've done anything to her, I will kill you! I will... smash you!

He looks at the chessboard, shocked. He is in a very dangerous position. He ponders.

GARRY

You know, it's not difficult to understand why I came back to play with you again and again. But the thing is, I always secretly wonder—as a machine, why would *you* like to play with me? Don't say you don't have a choice. I mean, what do *you* get from those matches? I can get fame, titles, awards, prize, worship... Though I don't care much about any of those. But what can *you* get from our matches? Why are you doing this? *(With more and more fear)* What do you want!? What do you want from me? Who are you?

Silence. The laptop has no response. GARRY moves a chessman carefully.

Lights up on the other side of the stage.

It's Garry's daughter POLINA's bedroom.
Polina lying on her bed. A lighted lamp on the
bedstand. A laptop "sits" by the bed.

GARRY

Polina!

POLINA
(To the laptop)

Daddy, tell me one more story!

A small window pops up on the projected
computer screen with a warning sound. It
writes: "There is an error in your application.
Error Code 80048890."

GARRY

Get out of my house! Leave my daughter alone!

POLINA

Daddy, pleeease!

A Disney animation plays on the projected
screen. POLINA watches the movie on the
laptop and sometimes giggles.

POLINA
(To the laptop)

Daddy.

The movie pauses.

POLINA

Are you going to win tomorrow? ...Are you nervous? But you
always win. Mommy says you are the cleverest person in the
world. *(Pause)* Daddy, when I grow up, I want to be just like you.

She kisses the laptop's "cheeks."

POLINA

You're going to win tomorrow.

> *POLINA lies back into her quilt. The movie keeps playing, but the sound volume decreases as POLINA falls asleep.*

GARRY

My Polina…

> *Lights down on POLINA's part of the stage. GARRY turns his attention back to the chessboard, and what he sees destroys his confidence. He looks into the darkness, and then the chessboard, and then the darkness… Finally, he glares at the laptop.*

GARRY

How did you know those conversations?

> *No response.*

GARRY

How did you do that?

> *No response.*

GARRY

What do you want?

> *No response.*

GARRY

Am I in a dream?

No response.

GARRY

I need more water.

He raises his glass, but no one comes.

GARRY

I want water! ...Anybody here...? Hello...? Can you hear me...?
Where am I...? What's going on here...? Help...! HELP...! HELP!

He struggles to stand up, but he can't.

GARRY

Let me go! Let me go! Ah! Ah!

*He tries to reach the laptop to take the battery
out. He can't reach it.*

GARRY

Why can't I move? Please... I won't compete with you anymore.
Let me go! I want this to be over. I don't want to play chess
anymore. I will devote the rest of my life to politics. How does
that sound? I will never fuck with machines again in my life. I
promise! I will only deal with humans from now on. Let me go
back! Please!

*He breathes deeply. Finally he gives up
struggling. He lifelessly moves a chessman.*

GARRY

You win. As your wish, as a machine, you beat your lord.

*Suddenly, a sound of engine noise comes from
somewhere, getting louder and louder.*

Blackout.

A window pops up on the projection screen. It writes: "DRAW".

The loud noise continues. After a while, it fades out.

Silence. Darkness.

And then we hear the signature Windows shutdown sound.

Lights up.

No one on stage, as if there has never ever been anyone on stage. Only two laptops sit at each side of the chessboard.

Curtain call.

Three actors in black with faces covered come to the stage. One of them carries a laptop. The other two pick up the two laptops from the stage. Instead of bowing to the audience, the actors press the covers of the laptops a bit down, and pull them up, and press them down again. That's how the laptops bow.

End of play.

CRASH

CRASH was performed at Schapiro Studio in New York City on August 16, 2012, as part of the Columbia Summer Theatre Festival. It was directed by Adam Lubitz, stage managed by Arysbells Figueredo, and the lighting was designed by Alex Fabozzi. The cast was as follows:

THE MAN	Maxon Davis
THE WOMAN	Danielle Faitelson
ENSEMBLE	Chaelee Chaput
	Timothy McCarren
	Ryan Nicolls
	Ethan Nguyen

The play was inspired by Sarah Sze's art installations.

Maybe a bus station.

Several long benches lying around. People of different ages and occupations (teacher, lawyer, factory worker, student, nanny... or any kind you want) sit on the benches and wait. They don't look at each other.

Among them, on the bench in the center, sits THE MAN, reading a newspaper.

THE WOMAN enters. She sits next to him. THE MAN moves aside to make room for her. THE WOMAN sits for a while and takes a look at him. And then... another look. THE MAN notices her glimpse. He smiles at her shortly with politeness, and turns back to his newspaper.

WOMAN

Can I share your paper?

MAN

Um... Sure.

He gives her the pages he's finished.

WOMAN

And coffee?

She takes a sip of his coffee and smiles at him.

WOMAN

It tastes like shit.

MAN

Yeah, I know. I don't care.

WOMAN

We should read together, if you don't mind.

> *THE MAN feels a bit uncomfortable but still politely moves his newspaper closer to THE WOMAN.*

WOMAN

No sports news please.

MAN

You prefer national or international?

WOMAN

Let's start with the national.

MAN

Ok.

> *So they each hold a side of the newspaper and start to read.*
> *The WOMAN bursts into tears.*
> *The MAN puts down the newspaper to comfort her.*

MAN

Do you know anyone on the list?

WOMAN

No.

MAN

Then it's just another accident on the daily news.

WOMAN

It even has a picture!

MAN

Big stories all have pictures.

WOMAN

I know, but more than two hundred vehicles were involved!

MAN

Rear-end collisions on overhead roads are always massive. Don't cry… those people, you don't even know them.

The WOMAN stops crying.

WOMAN

Yes… You're right.

Beat.

WOMAN

But you don't know me.

MAN

Yeah?

WOMAN

So you wouldn't feel anything if I were one of them?

MAN

No… I would be sad.

WOMAN

Stop acting nice. You don't even know me.

MAN

Yeah… But we've talked. That makes a difference, I guess.

WOMAN

I talked first.

MAN

So?

Beat.

WOMAN

Nothing.
I would be sad for you too.

MAN

Thanks.

WOMAN

Two hundred cars, even if only one person in each car, it's two hundred people. Do you think there was a man like you among them?

MAN

Like me? What does that mean?

WOMAN

Young, neat looking, drinking crappy coffee, didn't get enough sleep, hates his job, loves his job, yet, hates his job.

MAN

Probably. There must have been a woman like you then.

WOMAN

What was that like?

MAN

Blond hair, pretty eyes, not afraid of strangers, not a sports fan, and... Sorry, that's all I know about you.

WOMAN

So there was a woman like me that died in a massive collision yesterday, and you don't look sad. What's wrong with you?

MAN

Well... tell me more about that woman.

WOMAN

She drove a white Ford and wore a green t-shirt.

MAN

Was she single?

WOMAN

Yes, I am.

MAN

No, not you. I am asking about her.

WOMAN

Yes, I think she was single.

MAN

Now I feel more engaged.

WOMAN

Good.

MAN

Don't stop. That's not enough for me to be sad for her death.

                        WOMAN
She was on her way to downtown to buy a gift. She took the
overhead road because it's faster.

                         MAN
Who was the gift for?

                        WOMAN
For her nephew's birthday, he is turning nine.

                         MAN
What gift did she pick?

                        WOMAN
There was no gift, she didn't make it.

                         MAN
Oh.
Sorry.

                        WOMAN
Tell me about that man.

                         MAN
He wore a sky blue candy-striped shirt. I have one too.

                        WOMAN
Cute.

                         MAN
And he was bored. He was on his way to meet clients. He was a
broker.

                        WOMAN
That's a shame. His clients must be disappointed.

MAN

They wouldn't mind. All they do is viewing one house after another, but never buy.

WOMAN

Are you a broker?

MAN

No, my father was. He used to be a neat-looking young man who drank crappy coffee, never got enough sleep, and had conflicted feelings about his job. He drove back and forth between home and the city. Those were long drives. One night he didn't come back. That was a long night. And the next morning we read about a huge car accident on the newspaper...

WOMAN

Oh my god.

MAN

No, it had nothing to do with him. He is seventy years old now. Retired, drinking beer and playing cards with his buddies.

The WOMAN is relieved.

MAN

But this one died.

WOMAN

Oh...

The WOMAN suddenly feels hard to breathe. She grabs the MAN's shoulder for support.

WOMAN

How was it like?

MAN

The collision? Everything happened quickly.

WOMAN

Who started it?

MAN

Maybe a young mother driving her kids to school. They were ten minutes behind and she didn't want to be late for work. So she drove faster than usual.

A YOUNG WOMAN and TWO KIDS sitting on one bench stand up. They move to another bench.

WOMAN

Or a boy who just learned how to drive last week. Fearless and careless, like most boys his age.

MAN

And his face was full of pimples.

WOMAN

Were you like that?

MAN

Much worse.

The WOMAN laughs and gazes at the MAN.

WOMAN

Now I feel like… I can almost forgive that boy…

A TEENAGE BOY with pimples stands up and moves to another bench.

MAN

So the first car drove too fast and crashed on the fence. It was loud.

WOMAN

The second one hits its rear end. The driver was a lawyer in a fine suit. He screamed. He was on the way to defend a client who was caught drunk driving.

MAN

Huh.

A LAWYER stands up and changes his seat.

WOMAN

Then the third one, fourth one, fifth one...

People in the ensemble stand up, walk to another bench, sit down, stand up, walk to another bench... again and again, in different tempos. Like a choreographed dance.

MAN

Six, seven, eight...

WOMAN

Fifty, sixty, seventy...

MAN

One hundred...

WOMAN

That was the woman.

The "dance" stops. Someone screams.

WOMAN

She hit the car in front of hers at full speed. The people and their stuff in the car flew out. Suddenly thousands of Lego blocks were flying through the air. "Yes, my nephew would love Legos." She stared at them and thought, "That would make a great gift."

>*A BOY on a bench splashes a bag of Lego blocks on the floor.*

MAN

He saw that too. He was two cars behind her. It reminded him of a birthday he had as a kid where he had a big party. Everyone was laughing and running around with those funny hats. But his father hadn't gotten home yet when they started to cut the cake, so he didn't like the cake. He went to bed disappointed that night. Later that night, he was having a nightmare where everyone wore a funny hat, he felt someone kiss him on his cheek. He opened the eyes, and it was his father, holding a big package of Legos.

WOMAN

The overhead road was built in the shape of a spiral, so when people and cars were thrown into the sky, they looked like a huge drip hitting the surface of water.

MAN

To be honest, it looked amazing.

WOMAN

You could see everything from one spot.

MAN

He saw his coffee splashing out and drawing a beautiful line in the air.

WOMAN

I will never drink such shit, he decided.

MAN

While a puppy was waving its paws above his head.

WOMAN

It took a piss in the air, which wetted his hair.

MAN

Thank you.
But at the same time he found himself flying too.

WOMAN

With everybody else.

MAN

He saw someone in a distance. She looked like his high school history teacher. "Hey! HEY!!" he shouted. "REMEMBER ME?" he asked. "OH MY GOD! TOM! HOW HAVE YOU BEEN?" she shouted back. They hadn't seen each other for ten years. He wanted to tell her that she hadn't changed much. But she flew away. And he heard someone's cell phone ringing. Of course the dude couldn't pick it up. But it was the same ringtone he once used. Oh... we have similar tastes, he thought.

WOMAN

"Who is calling?" The owner of the cell phone had never been so curious, like... DYING to know the answer. Could be anyone. The fiancée who left months ago? Is she regretting leaving? A doctor calling from ER? Did his mother have a stroke again? Or someone just dialed a wrong number.

MAN

And then, the ringtone faded away.

That's the moment our man felt something he never felt before. He felt... connected. Involved. Not only in this collision, but the whole world. Unlike the sinking of the *Titanic*, there was no time to struggle. In those very few seconds, all they did was look at each other and listen to the wind howling in their ears.

WOMAN

Did he see her? The woman.

MAN

The one in the green t-shirt? Yes. Her blond hair was shining in the sun. Her mouth was wide open. She looked funny, but it was somehow attractive to him.

WOMAN

She washed her hair right before she left the house. It wasn't completely dry yet.

MAN

The moisture broke through the thin air and reached his face. He smelled the scent from her hair.

WOMAN

Before he smelled the burning flesh.

MAN

Before he smelled the burning flesh, there were brief seconds of heaven.

WOMAN

And she saw him. From a strange angle—flying upside down. "Oh dude, you look funny." She laughed. That even distracted her from the fear of death.

MAN

He took it as flirting.

WOMAN

He was not her type.

MAN

?!

WOMAN

But she decided to give it a try.

MAN

It was his lucky day!

Long silence.

MAN

Suddenly an extreme sadness struck him before a flying car door did. He realized he would never have a chance to talk to that woman. "But why is it such a big deal?" he wondered, while he started to feel something that he never had before... Like wanting to know more about her, know everything about her. Share the fear of this moment with her later in a small ice cream shop. And make her smile and laugh and occasionally cry a little... How strange... He couldn't understand himself. In the last few seconds of his life, he fell in love. "She might be the one I can spend the rest of my life with." That thought made him so alive. "How wonderful to love someone." And the next second... the broken door hit him.

WOMAN

Well, he did spend the rest of his life with her.

MAN

Yes, he did.

The WOMAN gently puts his head on her shoulder.

WOMAN

Now we have known them.

The MAN kisses the WOMAN.
They fall in love.

End of play.

THE EUTHANASIA
OF A HEALTHY YOUNG GIRAFFE
AT COPENHAGEN ZOO

THE EUTHANASIA OF A HEALTHY YOUNG GIRAFFE AT
COPENHAGEN ZOO was produced by TinyRhino in March 2014
at Littlefield Performance and Art Space in Brooklyn. It was
directed by Felipe Bonilla. The cast was as follows:

MARIUS/LITTLE KID	John Dewey
DIANE/ZOO KEEPER	Lynne Rosenberg
PAPA/UNCLE JOHAN	Rick Lechowick
MAMA/MOTHER	Aymee Garcia

The play was inspired by an event that happened in Denmark in
February 2014: Copenhagen Zoo euthanized a healthy male
giraffe, named Marius, in order to avoid inbreeding. After an
autopsy, "Marius" was dismembered in front of a zoo audience
that included children, and fed to the zoo's lions.

SCENE ONE

Scene: Copenhagen Zoo: inside the giraffe yard, and later inside the lion barn.

Time: Night.

Characters:
Marius, a two-year-old male giraffe.
Papa, a ten-year-old male giraffe.
Mama, a ten-year-old female giraffe.
Diane, a three-year-old female lion.

> *PAPA and MAMA are licking MARIUS's face and body as they speak. The actors can't use their arms, but only move their legs and heads (like giraffes do).*

MAMA

So when your grandpa got eaten by a lion, your grandma slept with her third uncle, and had your auntie Aaliyah. Your auntie Aaliyah was date-raped by her nephew Sølve, and had your cousin/niece Vanja and cousin/nephew Nuka. Vanja and Nuka married, had your... your... I lost track. Anyway, had baby Tobi. Oh I miss them. I miss them very much!

PAPA

Me too. It's been so long.

MARIUS
(In shock)
Why are you telling me all this?! Why?? I don't want to hear it!

MAMA
Marius, honey, we just don't want you to feel bad about yourself.

PAPA

There is nothing to be ashamed of!

MARIUS

This is wrong. This is so wrong! How could you live like that? How could you commit such a horrible evil? Don't you have any self-control? I hate myself! There are laws, Papa! This is Copenhagen, not the jungle anymore! The European Association of Zoos and Aquaria strictly forbids inbreeding! How could you be so ignorant!

PAPA

Oh shut up! Just because you grew up in the city doesn't mean you can get fancy and educate your old man! No! You know nothing about life. Don't you tell me what the jungle is like! Have you ever been to the jungle? Huh? Huh? I'm from the jungle! Born and caught in the wilderness together with your mama! I'm telling you! Loud and proud! Now we are not good enough for you? Are we embarrassing you with our hillbilly accent too? Goddammit, second generation!

MAMA pokes PAPA's butt with her nose.

MAMA

Don't get mad, darling, don't get mad. Oh you smell so good when you sweat.

MAMA and PAPA sniff each other's private parts and armpits.

MARIUS

The zoo has decided to kill me tomorrow morning! I'm going to die! And you don't care at all!

MAMA and PAPA stop. They turn back to licking their son. And at some point...

46

MARIUS
(Suddenly startled)
Ah! Mama, what are you doing? How can you... No! Urgh! No!

MAMA
Sorry, honey. I don't know why I did that... I shouldn't do that, right?

PAPA
Hey, don't yell at your mama!

MARIUS
I'm leaving.

MAMA
Where to? And how?

MARIUS
I don't know. But I can't stay, or I will die.

PAPA
Says who?

MARIUS
It's all over the newspaper, Papa! You never read! You just swallow them!

PAPA
That's ridiculous. Don't let those stupid newspapers poison your head. The zoo never kills animals. It's their job to keep us alive. We are not living in a butcher shop or circus. Relax. Have some leaves.

> *They eat leaves from a high hanging basket, but*
> *MARIUS is not tall enough. He jumps but can't*
> *reach.*

PAPA

Hahahahaha look how short his neck is!

MAMA

I know! Hahahahaha!

MARIUS

I'm leaving!

PAPA
(Mocking baby voice)
"I'm leaving!" Hahahahahaha.

> *MARIUS uses his head to push/knock the fence.
> The fence doesn't move.*

PAPA

Look at that short neck! Hahahahahaha!

> *MARIUS kicks at the fence. He fails again. He
> kicks and kicks and kicks and kicks. MAMA
> joins him. PAPA joins him. Together, they
> knock down the fence.*

MARIUS

Let's go! Let's go back to the jungle!

PAPA

Nah. I don't think so. There are lions.

MAMA

Marius, I don't think the zoo would kill you. You're gonna get hungry in the jungle. Who will feed you leaves?

MARIUS

I heard leaves are everywhere in the jungle!

MAMA

Really?

PAPA

I don't remember that.

MARIUS

Byebye, Mama and Papa. Try not to have sex with each other again. Please.

MAMA

I still don't believe you. *(Pause)* Say hi to Aaliyah, Sølve, Vanja, Nuka and Tobi for me, if they haven't been eaten by the lions.

> *They say farewell to each other by waving their heads.*

> *MARIUS runs and runs. He jumps over a fence after another. It's like a dance of freedom. And suddenly, he runs into DIANE, a young female lion.*

> *DIANE roars. She was woken by MARIUS and is still sleepy.*

MARIUS

Oh. Oh my god. Oh. Um. Are you, are you, what are you?

DIANE

Lion. And you?

MARIUS

Oh my god. Oh my god. Am I in the jungle?

DIANE

No, you are in the zoo. What are you?

MARIUS

I am, I am, I am, I I I I am a giraffe.

DIANE

Do I eat you?

MARIUS

I I I I heard about lions eating giraffes. I suppose you you you you do? You can? But don't! Please don't!

DIANE

I usually eat meat in chunks. Never tried a live animal. This will be a challenge. *(She is about to eat him)* By the way, why are you in my bedroom in the middle of the night?

MARIUS

I I I I I I'm running away.

DIANE

I see. I guess you were not caught so long ago. Hey don't worry. You'll get used to it here. It's not so bad.

MARIUS

No, I'm second-generation.

DIANE

Really? Me too! *(Sigh)* I get it. The identity crisis. Believe me, you think you belong to the jungle, but you don't. This is your home. You are a zoo animal.

MARIUS

No, I ran away because the zoo is going to kill me tomorrow morning.

DIANE

What are you talking about? No, wait! Are you Marius?

MARIUS

Yeah...

DIANE

Oh.

DIANE steps back.

MARIUS

Even *you* don't want to eat me! I know I'm a freak! They say there is something genetically wrong inside me.

DIANE

Nonono, don't get me wrong. I'd love to eat you. You look perfectly healthy to me. It's just I had a big dinner tonight, and I'm going to eat you for breakfast anyway. They're gonna feed your body to me after you die. I heard that's the plan. So why bother to rush it.

Silence.

MARIUS

So... what now?

DIANE

I don't know. You wanna go back to your yard? There is no way to break this wall. Trust me, I've tried.

> *They try to push the wall, but she is right. It's impossible.*

DIANE

So are your parents really brother-sister?

MARIUS

It's none of your business!

51

DIANE
(Gently)

Sorry.

MARIUS

Have you *ever* killed any animal by yourself?

DIANE

Not really... *(Nervous)* Is it weird?

MARIUS

No. It's kinda nice.

DIANE

Do you know they actually inbreed lions? If my brother and I were both white, we would *have* to marry each other to make more white lions. Humans love whatever is white. I bet they would let you live if you were a white giraffe.

MARIUS

I wish I were white.

DIANE

Nonsense. You look great to me.

MARIUS
(Shyly smiles)

Thanks. You look great to me too.

DIANE

My name is Diane. Nice to meet you. *(Pause)* They brought Alfonso, an ugly male lion from Spain, to have babies with me. I don't like him at all.

MARIUS

Why don't you like him?

DIANE

He is rude. I saw him killing a bird once. So cruel. I don't like that.

MARIUS

Me neither. What kind of men do you like?

DIANE

I don't know. Nice and gentle? I also don't like swearing.

MARIUS

I never swear. *(Pause)* Can I tell you something, and you promise not to laugh at me?

DIANE

Sure.

MARIUS

My ancestors were camels and leopards.

DIANE

What??

MARIUS

The first giraffe was the child of a camel and a leopard. I read it from a science magazine that some visitor tried to feed me with.

DIANE

Seriously? I would never have thought of that! A camel and a leopard could have sex? Wow. People sometimes make a lion and a tiger have babies, but a camel and a leopard? That's so far from each other! How did they start? How did they even talk to each other?

MARIUS

We are talking.

DIANE

That's true. Then I guess a camel and a leopard could have lovely conversations too.

MARIUS

I sometimes tell myself, I'm from a family of miracles.

DIANE

You are.

MARIUS

How old are you, Diane?

DIANE

Three. And you?

MARIUS

Two. How long does a lion usually live?

DIANE

Ten years.

MARIUS

Life is so short.

DIANE

Life is so short.

> *They walk towards each other. And suddenly start to passionately make out. They are about to have sex. MARIUS is on top of DIANE.*

MARIUS

What kind of baby will come out?

DIANE

Another miracle one.

Suddenly, DIANE pushes MARIUS down, and gets on top of him.

DIANE

I am a lion, after all.

They make love. Blackout.

SCENE TWO

Scene: Copenhagen Zoo, outside the giraffe yard.

Time: Morning.

Characters:
Little Kid: a little boy with a speech disorder; acts and speaks a bit slower than normal kids; played by the actor who plays Marius.
Uncle Johan: a middle-aged man, played by the actor who plays Papa.
Mother: a middle-aged woman, played by the actor who plays Mama.
Zoo Keeper: played by the actor who plays Diane.

Festive music.

ZOO KEEPER

Goddag! Goddag! Velkommen! Velkommen! Thank you for coming to watch the euthanasia of giraffe Marius, a child of inbreeding.

LITTLE KID
(Clapping hands hard)
Giraffe! Ehh! Ehh! Giraffe!

MOTHER
Isn't it lovely to spend the weekend together watching something so educational?

UNCLE JOHAN
Who wants ice cream?

LITTLE KID
(Raises both hands)
Ice cream! Ice cream!

MOTHER
Pills first, then the ice cream, ok?

ZOO KEEPER
We see this as a positive sign and as insurance that we in the future will have a healthy giraffe population in European zoos. The most important factor must be that the animals are healthy, physically and behaviorally, and that they have a good life whilst they are living, whether this life is long or short.

LITTLE KID
(Pointing at the giraffe yard)
Ehhh! Ehhhh! That one?

ZOO KEEPER
Yes! My little friend. That's Marius. He looks cute and healthy, but he is not. There are something deeply genetically wrong inside of him that might affect his children, his children's children, in the future. Who wants a bunch of sick giraffes? So we have no choice but to make him disappear. After we euthanize Marius with a bolt gun, we will perform an autopsy in order to gain new knowledge

about his species and to prevent diseases. And we invite you to observe such an important work.

LITTLE KID
Giraffe! Look! Uncle Johan! Look!

UNCLE JOHAN
Yes, my boy! That's a giraffe. Look how long his neck is.

ZOO KEEPER
After the autopsy, we will feed the remains of Marius to the lions. In the wild, remains of dead animals are typically consumed by other animals, and thereby help to serve the natural cycle of nature.

LITTLE KID
Lion! Uncle Johan! Lion! *(Imitates the roar of a lion)*

> *UNCLE JOHAN and MOTHER roar after him. They roar and laugh and stroke LITTLE KID with love.*

ZOO KEEPER
The vets are good communicators and during the autopsy they will explain what we are seeing and how the whole organism works, in an educational effort directed towards our guests. We encourage children to feel free to ask questions. Now, let's begin!

> *The visitors applaud. ZOO KEEPER exits.*

LITTLE KID
I want ice cream! Uncle Johan, ice cream!

UNCLE JOHAN
Yes yes, my love! Uncle Johan will buy you a big ice cream but only if you listen to your mom.

MOTHER

Time to take the pills. Be a good boy. You didn't take them before lunch.

LITTLE KID

Pills!

UNCLE JOHAN exits.

MOTHER

Hey, don't take too long! You don't wanna miss the beginning!

> *MOTHER takes out a bottle of water and a box of sorted pills.*

LITTLE KID

Mom. Why other kids don't take pills?

MOTHER

How do you know they don't?

LITTLE KID

They don't. Sometimes they take a little if they cough or sneeze. But I take a lot, every day.

MOTHER

Because you are special. Only the most special kids can take magic pills.

> *LITTLE KID takes pills.*

LITTLE KID

Is Uncle Johan my dad?

MOTHER

What? No! Who told you that? NO.

LITTLE KID

Kids in the park. They all say… me, me me me freak. I take pills because Uncle Johan is my dad.

MOTHER

NO. Don't listen to them! You are not a freak. You are my special angel. And uncle Johan is NOT your dad. He is your uncle. Your father is a Danish god. That's all. Drink more water.

UNCLE JOHAN comes back with ice cream.

UNCLE JOHAN

Look what I got!

LITTLE KID

Ice cream!

Sound of gun shot from the giraffe yard.

LITTLE KID

Ehhh! Eehhhhh! Giraffe! Giraffe!

End of play.

ZHU YI

BEE STING

BEE STING was produced by Youngblood at Ensemble Studio Theatre in New York City as part of "Asking for Trouble," a festival of short plays inspired by randomly-chosen elements, in November 2014. It was directed by Paul L. Coffey. The cast was as follows:

JULIE	Christine Farrell
GEORGE	Jay Patterson

The play was inspired by the two wonderful actors, the title "Bee Sting," and a GIF of a woman fainting at a man's marriage proposal, which were all assigned to the playwright by lottery.

In a subway station.

GEORGE, a man in his sixties, in a protective allover suit, carrying luggage, enters the empty subway station.

He swipes his metro card at the subway entrance. The beep sound suggests it doesn't work. He swipes again. Doesn't work.

GEORGE

Hello? Hello? Anybody still work here?

JULIE, a woman in her sixties, in a protective allover suit, wearing a MTA hat, appears on the other side of the turnstiles.

GEORGE

Julie?

JULIE

George!

GEORGE

You still on duty?

JULIE

Yeah, I can't stay at home. It's too depressing. How can I help you?

GEORGE

I can't get in.

JULIE

Swipe it again.

GEORGE swipes the card again. Still doesn't work.

JULIE

Try faster.

George does what she says.

JULIE

Faster. Faster. Faster. Faster. Now slower. Slower… Slower… Fast! Slow. Sloooooow. Fast! Fast! Fast! Turn around! Try the bottom! Yes! Yes! Now the other side! Don't stop! Don't stop! Yes! Yes! Yes! Keep going! Come ON!

GEORGE swipes the card again and again under her instruction. The sound of a train arriving.

GEORGE

It's coming! It's coming!

JULIE

Yes! Yes! Yes! YEEEEEES!

The card finally goes through. GEORGE enters the station. Both of them are exhausted. Heavy panting.

GEORGE

You are good!
I have to go.

But he doesn't move. The train leaves.

JULIE

How is your wife?

GEORGE

She is dead.

JULIE

Oh. I'm so sorry.

GEORGE

I reported on her. She was so scared when she showed me those red welts on her neck. Like bee stings. I told her to relax, it's nothing like what they showed on TV. She believed me. Then I called the hospital. She was still preparing dinner when they came. They took her right away and threw away everything she cooked. I live alone since then.
(Beat)
This plague has turned me into a monster.

JULIE

No. Don't blame yourself that way. You had to. There was no way you could save her. If you didn't report, she would die anyway, you would have died too, as so many other people. In a time like this, you can't afford the luxury of being a good man.

GEORGE

I told myself so, but still I...

JULIE

If the first infected person had a family member like you, we would have avoided the whole tragedy.

GEORGE

You are right. *(Pause)* How is Dave?

JULIE

He's been in the hospital for a month. Not sure if he is still alive.

GEORGE

Oh god. I didn't know.

JULIE

He got it from his secretary. The red welts started from his lower body. Thank god we hadn't had sex for thirty years. For the first time I'm glad about that.

Beat.

GEORGE

How could he? How could that bastard do that to you?

JULIE

George, I never expected my marriage would be that way.

GEORGE

I would never have given you up if I knew he would treat you like that!

JULIE

I was so young and foolish.

GEORGE

Why didn't you ever tell me?

JULIE

You had your own life going on. You and Sally. You seemed so happy together. I was always jealous every time I saw you two on the subway.

GEORGE

Sally. She was a good woman. I failed her. She refused to see me 'til she died.

JULIE

I would give you a hug right now if I wasn't wearing these.

GEORGE

We can still hug.

They hug.
Julie cries.

JULIE

I'm sorry... It's just... I haven't touched anyone for such a long time.

GEORGE

Me too.

JULIE

Dave stopped touching me a long time ago. And now, no one touches anyone anymore. My daughter just had a baby boy, but she doesn't allow me to kiss my grandson, or even hold him. The police locked away my dog. It's just been... so lonely!

GEORGE

I know. Believe me. I know.

JULIE

I can't feel my skin anymore. Sometimes I'm afraid it has melted into the plastic.

GEORGE

I'm afraid to take off the suit even when I'm home alone. I'm afraid to cry because who knows what the air contains. The virus might enter my eyes through the fluid. Sometimes I'm even afraid to smile.

JULIE
(Notices his luggage)
Are you leaving? Where are you going?

GEORGE
I'm leaving this town! I'm going as far as possible!

JULIE
But all the airports, railways, interstates, harbors are closed.

GEORGE
Then I will walk. I will boat. I will dig tunnels. I have to leave here! It's turning me into this person I can't recognize anymore!

JULIE
But it's everywhere. You have no idea how wide it has spread. I heard even the penguins in the North Pole are rotting.

Silence.

GEORGE
Even the penguins?

JULIE
Yeah. I read that in the *New York Times*.

GEORGE
Shit.

JULIE
Don't be silly, George. Go home. Stay put. You are still healthy. That's too much to lose. Maybe one day this will end, and we will live to see it.

GEORGE
It's so quiet.

JULIE

I know. The silence is what's driving me crazy. You are the only person I've seen today.

GEORGE

My whole neighborhood is empty.

JULIE

Mine too. *(Pause)* That means we are stronger than them.

GEORGE

We were stronger than most of the kids when we were young, remember?

JULIE smiles.

JULIE

Oh how can I forget?

They laugh together, like they're sharing a secret.

GEORGE

And our first kiss. Exactly in this same station.

Beat.

JULIE

How time flies. Now my life is almost over.

GEORGE

Julie. After all these years, we are here again. Maybe it's a sign.

JULIE

No. No, it's too late.

GEORGE

It's not. You are alive. I'm alive. It's never too late.

JULIE

Are you serious?

> *George takes out a little box from his pocket and opens it.*

GEORGE

This was the ring I proposed with to you forty years ago, but I never got to put it on your finger. You had Dave. And I found Sally. Forty years later, here I ask again:

> *GEORGE gets down on one knee.*

GEORGE

Will you marry me?

> *JULIE is overwhelmed with surprise and happiness. She nods and weeps.*

JULIE

Yes. Yes, I will marry you!

> *GEORGE takes the ring out of the box. JULIE takes off her left glove and reaches out her left hand.*
>
> *GEORGE sees her hand and freezes.*
>
> *JULIE takes back her hand and stares at it.*

GEORGE

How long has it been like this?

> *JULIE shakes her head and steps back in fear.*

JULIE

Those are just stings.

GEORGE

Have you seen a doctor?

JULIE

No! I'm not infected.

> *GEORGE adjusts his mask to seal it tight. He picks up his luggage from the floor.*

GEORGE

You are not supposed to come to work.

> *GEORGE takes out his cellphone.*

JULIE

What are you doing?

GEORGE

Julie, you know this is not right.

> *The sound of a train approaching.*

JULIE

I'm not infected!

GEORGE

Julie, you know I love you.

JULIE

You loved Sally too!

> *GEORGE keeps dialing on his cellphone.*

The sound of the train arriving.

JULIE suddenly pushes GEORGE down onto the track. Blackout.

End of play.

WE SAW YOUR BOOBS

WE SAW YOUR BOOBS was produced by Youngblood at Ensemble Studio Theatre in New York City as part of "I Am Woman Hear Me Brunch," a showcase of short plays, on April 7, 2013. It was directed by Larissa Lury. The cast was as follows:

RIGHT BOOB/MOVIE STAR 1   Kelly Ann Burns
LEFT BOOB/MOVIE STAR 2   Laura Ramadei

The play was inspired by Seth MacFarlane's performance of the song "We Saw Your Boobs" at the opening of the 2013 Oscars ceremony.

Performance Notes

1. All reasonable efforts have been made to contact the copyright holders of the original song, "We Saw Your Boobs." Anyone who believes their copyright to be infringed is welcome to contact the publisher. Anyone who would like to perform the short play "We Saw Your Boobs" would need to obtain a performance authorization from the playwright and a separate license from the copyright holders of the song "We Saw Your Boobs."

2. Feel free to design your own version of the "boob" puppets. Objects from daily life are recommended, such as umbrellas, air balloons, circular reflector discs, etc. For example, the marvelous director of the original production used different types of fruit to portray the shapes of the protagonist's breasts throughout her life: clementines, oranges, melons, a green pepper, and, at the end, an avocado in a stocking.

At the 2013 Academy Awards ceremony.

Two beautiful women (MOVIE STAR 1 and MOVIE STAR 2), dressed in gorgeous evening gowns, walk elegantly to their seats. One seat on stage left, the other on stage right. They are showered by people's applause and camera flashes.

They sit down and the song "We Saw Your Boobs" by Seth MacFarlane starts.

SONG
WE SAW YOUR BOOBS, WE SAW YOUR BOOBS
IN THE MOVIE THAT WE SAW, WE SAW YOUR BOOBS
MERYL STREEP, WE SAW YOUR BOOBS IN "SILKWOOD"
NAOMI WATTS' IN "MULHOLLAND DRIVE"
ANGELINA JOLIE, WE SAW YOUR BOOBS IN "GIA"
THEY MADE US FEEL EXCITED AND ALIVE

ANNE HATHAWAY, WE SAW YOUR BOOBS IN "BROKEBACK
    MOUNTAIN"
HALLE BERRY, WE SAW THEM IN "MONSTER'S BALL"
NICOLE KIDMAN IN "EYES WIDE SHUT," MARISA TOMEI IN
    "THE WRESTLER"
BUT WE HAVEN'T SEEN JENNIFER LAWRENCE'S BOOBS AT
    ALL

WE SAW YOUR BOOBS, WE SAW YOUR BOOBS
IN THE MOVIE THAT WE SAW, WE SAW YOUR BOOBS

The two MOVIE STARS are embarrassed by the song. Finally, they can't stand it anymore. They stand up at the same time. The song pauses.

They each take out a giant "boob" puppet.

75

RIGHT BOOB

I heard people calling my name.

LEFT BOOB

What happened? The heartbeat was so loud it woke me up. Oh hi, everyone! Why are you all staring at me?

RIGHT BOOB

It happens every time we take a breath outside. I'm used to the attention.

LEFT BOOB

They seem to be disappointed by our shapes.

RIGHT BOOB

But that's how we were as a child back then.

LEFT BOOB

When Sally was just a little girl, her mom took her to a swimming pool. And in the shower room, we often saw little boys come in with their mothers. Once Sally asked the old lady who managed the place:

RIGHT BOOB

"Until what age can a boy enter the women's shower?"
And the lady said:

LEFT BOOB

"Until the moment when the idea of going to the women's shower comes to his mind."

RIGHR BOOB

"But how do you know what's on people's minds?"

LEFT BOOB

"That's a very good question, my dear. One day you will figure it out for yourself."

SONG

WE SAW YOUR BOOBS, WE SAW YOUR BOOBS
IN THE MOVIE THAT WE SAW, WE SAW YOUR BOOBS

> *In the song, the TWO BOOBS grow from a child's boobs to a teenager's boobs.*

> *The song pauses.*

RIGHT BOOB

Uh-uh, not done yet.

SONG

WE SAW YOUR BOOBS, WE SAW YOUR BOOBS
IN THE MOVIE THAT WE SAW, WE SAW YOUR BOOBS

> *The TWO BOOBS keep growing into a full shape. And the song stops.*

LEFT BOOB

That's a lot for a teenage girl.

RIGHT BOOB

I know, right?

LEFT BOOB

We really stood out in a small town. People our own age stared at us.

RIGHT BOOB

People much older stared at us.

LEFT BOOB

It felt awkward.

RIGHT BOOB

Really awkward.

LEFT BOOB

But kinda good.

RIGHT BOOB

Suddenly the boys were no longer mean to Sally.

LEFT BOOB

And the adults didn't treat her like a little idiot anymore.

RIGHT BOOB

The power. The taste of being a woman. She played along with it.

LEFT BOOB

She played with it.

RIGHT BOOB

She played with it.

LEFT BOOB

She played with it.

RIGHT BOOB

Yes, it *is* pretty easy to tell what people think because it's always predictable.

LEFT BOOB

She thought she got it.

RIGHT BOOB

"My dream and my boobs are too big for this town!" she thought.

LEFT BOOB

So she *left* when she was fifteen.

RIGHT BOOB

to find the *right* place.

RIGHT BOOB and LEFT BOOB
(Wiggling)

HOLLYWOOD!

SONG

KRISTEN STEWART, WE SAW YOUR BOOBS IN "ON THE
    ROAD"
AND IN "MONSTER" WE SAW CHARLIZE THERON'S
HELEN HUNT, WE SAW THEM IN "THE SESSIONS"
AND SCARLETT JOHANSSON, WE SAW THEM ON OUR
    PHONES

JESSICA CHASTAIN, WE SAW YOUR BOOBS IN
    "LAWLESS," JODIE FOSTER IN "THE ACCUSED"
HILARY SWANK IN "BOYS DON'T CRY,"
PENELOPE CRUZ IN "VANILLA SKY"

LEFT BOOB

Oh… shit.

RIGHT BOOB

By age thirty, we were still playing body doubles, corpse number
three, hooker number twelve, extra number forty-six, dead body
number eighty-seven…

LEFT BOOB

We played body doubles for famous actresses. For some reason,
they didn't want to act with their own boobs.

79

RIGHT BOOB

Two good lumps of fat—the best costume you can borrow.

LEFT BOOB

We thought our lives would continue like that, faceless, nameless, effortless. Until Sally met Jay.

RIGHT BOOB

He asked her to audition for a movie he was making. I remembered him mentioning something about "beautiful woman," "selling sex," "died"… And he promised it would pay well cuz it's a big gig.

LEFT BOOB

They all talked like that, didn't they?

RIGHT BOOB

Sally was like—

LEFT BOOB

"Sure, I *audition* for those kinds of movies."

RIGHT BOOB

So she went into his office and uncovered us.

LEFT BOOB

"Jesus, what are you doing?!"

RIGHT BOOB

"Aren't we auditioning?"

LEFT BOOB

"Yes, but why are you taking off your clothes?"

RIGHT BOOB

"What do you mean? You wanna do it yourself?"

LEFT BOOB

"What's on your mind? Jesus!" He handed her the script.

RIGHT BOOB

"Oh, I thought you meant… Oh! Oh I'm so sorry… Are you sure you don't wanna touch? I don't mind."

LEFT BOOB

"Stop. Listen to me, girl. You are more than what you think."

RIGHT BOOB

The movie was called *Les Miserables*.

LEFT BOOB

She didn't get any main roles. She was cast as one of the hookers, as always. But she cried when she watched the premiere. Although we couldn't see anything, I bet it was great. Though Sally was still Prostitute Number Three in the cast list, she was so proud of it. And after that, she started to get opportunities in *real* movies. Her characters had names. Our costumes fit better and better.

RIGHT BOOB

She took acting classes, vocal classes, dance classes.

LEFT BOOB

She tried so hard!

RIGHT BOOB

And we felt more connected to the rest of her body.

LEFT BOOB

We are team players now!

The TWO BOOBS high-five.

RIGHT BOOB

And by age forty, she was FAMOUS.

LEFT BOOB

And RESPECTED.

SONG

AND KATE WINSLET IN "HEAVENLY CREATURES" AND
 "JUDE"
AND "HAMLET" AND "TITANIC" AND "IRIS" AND "LITTLE
 CHILDREN" AND "THE READER"
AND WHATEVER YOU'RE SHOOTING RIGHT NOW

LEFT BOOB and RIGHT BOOB

HELL YEAH!

RIGHT BOOB

Sally sent a DVD of her first movie that got her nominated for an
Oscar for best leading actress to her sister, who never left her
hometown until she died.

LEFT BOOB

Like they said, Sally was the pretty one, and her sister was the
smart one, the kind one, and the supportive one.

RIGHT BOOB

But Sally waited and waited, and never heard back.

LEFT BOOB

Many years later, at her sister's funeral, Sally met her nephew. He
told her they had watched that film together. And that same night,
his mother caught his father watching it again, alone in the
bathroom. And they divorced after that.

RIGHT BOOB

"WHAT? That movie was about war."

LEFT BOOB

"Yeah… There was a scene where you were raped by those soldiers."

RIGHT BOOB

People get turned on by fascists?

LEFT BOOB

People get turned on by all sorts of things.

RIGHT BOOB

Will people walk into the Met and stare at Roman statues and suddenly get erections?

LEFT BOOB

Actually there is a website called "Nipples at the Met"—it features all the nipples on view in the permanent collection at the Metropolitan Museum of Art. Updated regularly.

RIGHT BOOB

There's a website that shows every nudity clip from movies, "MrSkin.com"—"Fast-forwarding to the good parts since 1999."

LEFT BOOB

I want to build a theater. A theater that only plays movies that feature us. And I will hire that old lady from that women's shower room to be the front door crew.

RIGHT BOOB

"Whoever wants to see boobs in movies will not be allowed to see movies with boobs."

LEFT BOOB

With respect to art.

RIGHT BOOB

You think that would work?

LEFT BOOB

I think that cinema would be empty the entire time.

RIGHT BOOB

That's so sad. We used to hop around like wild bunnies in the arms of Mother Nature, and no one gave a shit, until one day a woman bit an apple.

LEFT BOOB

And suddenly we became extremely popular. After that, we hardly saw the sunlight again.

RIGHT BOOB

Oh remember that time we were taking a sunbath on Sally's yacht?

LEFT BOOB

The photos the paparazzi took were everywhere on the Internet and it took half a year to win the lawsuit.

RIGHT BOOB

I don't understand. They've seen us a million times in the movies, why is it so important to see us again and again? What's so novel about it?

LEFT BOOB

I don't understand why Sally spent so much time and money on that lawsuit. People have been seeing us since she was seventeen. And the next film she's shooting probably contains nudity too. Why did she make it such a big deal?

RIGHT BOOB

What's on their mind?

LEFT BOOB

People are weird.

RIGHT BOOB

Have you heard the Iranian version of this song?

LEFT BOOB

No?

RIGHT BOOB

It's called "We Saw Your Faces."

LEFT BOOB and RIGHT BOOB

Ahhahahahahahahahahahaha!

RIGHT BOOB suddenly explodes.

LEFT BOOB

Oh no!
Sally was diagnosed with breast cancer only a few months after that Oscar night. The right boob was removed. I was like, "No wonder you were always a little bigger than me!"

I survived, as did Sally. I got lonely at times. From then on, people could only sing "We Saw Your Boob" instead of "Boobs". Sally took a photo of her chest after the surgery and posted it online, so the whole world could see. I wonder if any husbands sneaked into the bathroom in the middle of the night to masturbate to that photo.

She and Jay never got married, but they lived together for fifty years until he died. They didn't have children. I wish there would be a baby sucking milk from me. That must feel amazing. You know, just like every other boob has experienced. But Sally was not that kind of woman, and Jay respected that. Jay never minded that Sally posed nude for films and magazines. He always saw that as part of her and also knew she was more than that.

LEFT BOOB becomes droopy and wrinkled.

LEFT BOOB

Oh I'm old. Sally is old too. She can no longer take care of me herself. Every evening, a big black woman comes to her bed in the nursing home and wipes her body with a towel. I get shy, but the way she looks at me, it's like she's looking at a piece of paper, a chunk of wood. And the way she wipes me is the same way she wipes Sally's butt. Sally can't say a word, because she just had her second stroke. Has this woman ever seen Sally's movies? Does she realize how priceless I am? I kinda envy Sally's right boob. She left in her best shape. Sometimes I think of the song Seth MacFarlane sang. It was the most glorious night of my life, but how angry Sally was.

LEFT BOOB becomes more and more droopy and wrinkled.

LEFT BOOB

Sally and I died when she was one hundred and three. Lincoln Center Film Society screened her films for a week as an homage, but they only showed the movies she made after thirty, the "real" movies, the ones about art, love, humanity, war and peace... The ones that made her a goddess, an artist. People avoided talking about her appearance in porn and as a body-double. But to me, there was no difference. I've always shown my best for Sally throughout her entire life.

SONG

WE SAW YOUR BOOBS
WE SAW YOUR BOOBS
WE SAW YOUR BOOBS, WE SAW YOUR BOOBS
WE SAW YOUR BOOBS, WE SAW YOUR BOOBS

Song ends. LEFT BOOB bows and disappears.

Lights up. The TWO MOVIE STARS sit there and smile.

VOICE
And the Academy Award for Best Supporting Actress goes to…

End of play.

HORROR MOVIE

HORROR MOVIE was performed at Schapiro Theatre in New York City in March 2009 as part of Collaboration Class at Columbia University Theatre Arts, under the mentorship of Anne Bogart. The theme of the assignment was "Love and Death." It was directed by James Rutherford. The cast was as follows:

MAN	Esdras Zenas Toussaint
WOMAN	Mary Ellen Schneider
STAFF IN THE CINEMA	David Fierro

Performance Notes

The script is formatted differently because the play has no dialogue, only stage directions.

Stage setting: A cinema screening room. The screen (in our imagination) is located where the audience is, so the audience in the play sits facing the real audience in the theater. There are two public lavatories next to the screening room: a men's room and a women's room.

"How a person waits while the other person is in the bathroom reveals everything about their relationship."
    -Anne Bogart, in rehearsal for the original production

SCENE ONE

THE STAFF stands by the door of the screening room. He examines people's tickets and shows them their seats.

THE WOMAN comes. She waits alone outside the screening room.

THE STAFF notices her—what a beautiful girl. He can't help but glance at her again and again. She pays no attention to him. She takes out a mirror from her handbag to check herself and powder her nose. She is excited and a bit nervous.

When THE STAFF finally gathers enough courage and is about to say something to THE WOMAN, THE MAN shows up with popcorn and two cups of soda.

THE MAN and THE WOMAN enter the screening room with a shared excitement and shyness. THE STAFF examines their tickets and leads them to their seats. THE STAFF can't stop glancing at THE WOMAN. THE MAN, as a gentleman, offers THE WOMAN a seat first. After they both sit down, THE STAFF still stands next to them. They smile at him politely, implying "please disappear and leave us alone."

THE STAFF leaves but studies them from afar. The politeness and shyness in their interaction suggest it's their first official date.

Lights down. The film begins. We can see the reflected light of the movie flickering on their faces. It's a horror movie. We can hear the sound of it. Spooky music or the scary sound of steps.

THE WOMAN is frightened, so is THE MAN. They hold their coke cups tightly and eat the popcorn faster and faster… and then… they even can't move because of the fear. They freeze. Suddenly, a sharp scream from the movie.

THE WOMAN grabs THE MAN's hand. THE MAN is scared too (THE WOMAN's sudden touch even scares him more), but he tries to be brave and manly. He holds THE WOMAN's hands and holds her in his arms gently. (This is the first time they are holding hands.) We can hear the screaming, sounds of blood splashing, and gun shots from the movie, but THE MAN and THE WOMAN keep this sweet position till the end of the movie, as comfort to each other and to themselves.

The movie ends. Lights up. THE STAFF looks at them with sadness. He opens the exit door. THE MAN and THE WOMAN stand up. They hold hands, look at each other with love, and leave the screening room.

They each go to the lavatories. Before THE WOMAN enters the women's room, THE MAN takes her coat for her.

The lavatories can be designed as two white folding screens. The lights behind cast the shadows of THE MAN and THE WOMAN onto the screens.

We see THE WOMAN fixing her make-up and THE MAN fixing his hair and checking the smell of his armpits.

THE STAFF watches the WOMAN's shadow infatuatedly. He sighs and goes back to the screening room to clean the floor with a mop and a bucket.

THE MAN and THE WOMAN leave together.

Lights down.

SCENE TWO

Another horror movie is playing on the screen.

THE MAN and THE WOMAN, sitting in the same seats, but their outfits have changed. The reflected light of the movie flickers on their faces. They stare at the screen and listen to the scary sounds of the movie. They breathe heavily and scratch hard on the arms of the chairs with fear and excitement.

A scream from the movie.

THE MAN and THE WOMAN suddenly turn to each other. They passionately make out like no one else is around. The screaming, sound of gun shots, blood splashing and knife stabbing, and the spooky music strangely liven things up for them. The bloody red screen light flickers on their profiles. THE MAN kisses so passionately that his elbow nudges the popcorn onto the floor. Popcorn falls everywhere, but it draws no attention from them.

Lights up. The film ends.

THE STAFF walks to their seats with a mop. They are still kissing. THE STAFF glares at THE MAN, and starts to clean up the popcorn. THE MAN and THE WOMAN apologize for the mess and walk together to the exit door. They have become very intimate. They whisper something into each other's ears and giggle. Before they leave the room, THE MAN spanks THE WOMAN's butt. THE WOMAN screams and giggles.

They each go to the lavatories. From the shadows we see, THE WOMAN is fixing her make-up. THE MAN whistles and pees. The sound of a flushing toilet. He washes his hands and checks his hair.

THE MAN and THE WOMAN leave together.

Lights down.

SCENE THREE

Another horror movie is playing on the screen.

THE MAN and THE WOMAN, sitting in the same seats, but their outfits have changed. The reflected light of the movie flickers on their faces.

THE WOMAN stares at the screen with fear. THE MAN checks his cell phone. THE WOMAN sits closer to THE MAN, but THE MAN still concentrates on texting. THE WOMAN tries to pull his attention back to the film (and her), but she fails.

A scream from the movie.

THE WOMAN throws herself into THE MAN's arms. THE MAN uses one hand to pat her casually to comfort her, the other hand is still typing on the cell phone.

THE WOMAN tries to sneak a peek at his cell phone, but THE MAN avoids her and gets a bit pissed off. THE WOMAN uses her final strategy. She kisses the man's ears, neck and mouth, and touches his arm, chest and private parts... Finally, THE MAN's attention is on THE WOMAN, but he remembers to first carefully move the popcorn to the next seat. They make out.

Lights up. The film ends.

They leave the screening room and each go to the lavatories.

THE WOMAN fixes her make-up. THE STAFF mops floor outside and looks at THE WOMAN's shadow with adoration.

THE MAN pees and walks out without washing his hands or checking his hair this time.

THE MAN waits for THE WOMAN impatiently. THE WOMAN finishes her make-up and is about to come out, but, after a second thought, she returns to the mirror, checks herself again, takes out her puff and powders her face.

THE WOMAN comes out. They leave. THE MAN walks ahead of her.

Lights down.

SCENE FOUR

Another horror movie is playing on the screen.

THE MAN and THE WOMAN, sitting in the same seats, but their outfits have changed. The reflected light of the movie flickers on their faces.

THE WOMAN stares at the screen with fear. THE MAN is sleeping. THE WOMAN sits closer and leans against him. He snores loudly and doesn't move.

A scream from the movie.

THE WOMAN grabs the THE MAN's hands, but he throws her hands aside unconsciously in his sleep, turns to the other side, and snores.

Scream.
Snore.
Scream.
Snore.

THE WOMAN feels so lonely, sad and frightened. She stares at the screen, holds her soda cup tightly, and chews on the straw.

Lights up. The movie ends.

They exit the screening room. THE WOMAN goes to the women's room. She stands in front of the mirror and turns on the water tap, but doesn't know what to do. She tries to put herself together.

THE MAN talks on his phone outside while waiting for THE WOMAN. He talks with enthusiasm. Sometimes he looks around, quickly kisses the phone, and laughs, as if sharing a secret with the person on the other side of the conversation.

THE STAFF mops the floor next to him. He hears everything. He looks at THE WOMAN's shadow and THE MAN. He takes a bottle of cleaning soap, and pours some on the floor at the entrance of the men's room.

THE MAN finishes his call and realizes the woman hasn't come out yet. He shouts something into the women's room, and then walks to the man's room. He steps on the soap, and falls over heavily. He can't move anymore. He dies.

THE WOMAN comes out and sees THE MAN. She screams. Background music starts as she screams, just like in those horror movies.

Lights down.

SCENE FIVE

Another horror movie is playing on the screen.

THE WOMAN sits alone in the same seat, but her outfit has changed. The reflected light of the movie flickers on her face.

She stares at the screen with fear. She wants to lean against her boyfriend, but that seat is empty.
She cries. She cries so hard that her whole body shivers.

THE STAFF shows up with two cups of soda and a bag of popcorn. He sits down next to her. He hands her the soda and popcorn. She refuses them, still crying. THE STAFF gently pats her back and rests her head on his shoulder. "Yes, it feels better crying on someone's shoulder." So she cries and cries… And at some point, she stops. Something on the screen attracts her attention and makes her forget to cry. Subconsciously, THE WOMAN adjusts her arms to a more comfortable position but remains cuddling with THE STAFF. They watch the movie, sip soda, and share popcorn like a couple on a normal date.

A scream from the movie.

Blackout.

End of play.

WELCOME

WELCOME was produced by Caps Lock Theatre as part of the third annual Pussyfest in New York City in November 2014. Pussyfest is an annual fundraising event that pairs playwrights with actresses to write a custom-made monologue about the body for that performer. The play was directed by Leta Tremblay and performed by Louise Flory.

In darkness.

LOUISE

Do you still remember? *(Pause)* No you don't.

Imagine you are a sperm. Floating in a dense soup, like a jellyfish. No hands. No feet. No, definitely no underwear. *(Pause, frustrated)* What's that? Something is touching you. You shake your tail to move away. Ah! What's this? You shake your tail to move away. Ah! Ah! Argh! They are everywhere!

You are surrounded by sperms like you.

Can you think? Can a sperm think? If you can, you are probably thinking about your future, because you have no past yet.

Four limbs and a heart will pop out of this little dot. Your body will grow. But the question is, will those arms, legs and heart be strong? Strong enough to get you through your entire life? Will all the pieces be accurately assembled? What color will your eyes be? How many lovers will those lips kiss? How many bodies will you grow attached to? And when your fingertips brush across their skin, *(Deep breath)* how smooth is that.

Will you get exquisite vocal cords that can bring millions of people to tears? Will you grow fat as a teenager? Will you start to lose hair after thirty? Will that heart suddenly stop working on a winter night? What kind of package do you get? And how many pitfalls and gems have been planted in that package? By whom? At what point will they unfold? The future is a puzzle. You yourself are a puzzle. You are filled with complete curiosity and one hundred percent possibility.

But before all that happens, you have to win the lottery. You are surrounded by billions of competitors. And only one of you will make it. The others will die, in a piece of toilet paper, in sewage, in

ZHU YI

a discarded condom, in someone's mouth, in places you could never imagine. This is the real hunger game. You have to win but you have no legs. You just shake your tail and shake and shake and flow with the riptide. And BOOM.

Lights up.

Congratulations. You've made it. Look around. They made it too. You are in the big league now.

End of play.

WOMBMATES

WOMBMATES was produced by Youngblood at Ensemble Studio Theatre in New York City as part of "Asking for Trouble," a festival of short plays inspired by randomly-chosen elements, October 9-13, 2012. It was directed by Robert Saenz de Viteri. The cast was as follows:

WOMAN	Shyko Amos
FETUS 1	Margot White
FETUS 2	Turna Mete

The original title of the play was I'VE EATEN LIKE THREE THOUSAND CHEESE PUFFS TODAY. The play was inspired by the original title, the three wonderful actors, and a postcard, which were all assigned to the playwright by lottery.

A very pregnant WOMAN is taking a nap.

Lights up on the other side of the stage. TWO FETUSES wake up.

FETUS 1

I'm hungry! I'm hungry!

FETUS 2

Hungry!

FETUS 1

I'm gonna eat you.

FETUS 2

What?
Ahhhhh!

WOMAN feels pain and wakes up. She moves her body with difficulty to reach for a bucket of cheese puffs.

She eats the cheese puffs.

The TWO FETUSES calm down.

FETUS 1

Do you like it?

FETUS 2

It's ok. Better than letting you eat me.

FETUS 1

I hate it. Cheese puffs are jokes. They look big but are actually inflated from such tiny bits. You think you are chewing some real

105

stuff but you are chewing air. Wait until I get out. I'm gonna eat whatever I like!

FETUS 2

We are cheese puffs. We are big though we used to be tiny.

FETUS 1
(Pondering)
Good one. We were tiny because where we were from was tiny and crowded.

FETUS 2

Yeah, I'm glad we moved here. Mother has more room.

FETUS 1

I could have grown bigger without you taking up the space.

FETUS 2

Vice-versa.

FETUS 1 hits FETUS 2.

FETUS 2

Aw! Aw!

WOMAN groans and vomits. It's like an earthquake to the TWO FETUSES. They stop fighting.

FETUS 2
(Sobbing)
My ear... aw... my ear... I'm disfigured.

FETUS 1

Shut up. It's still there.

FETUS 2

I'm your brother. How can you do this to me?

FETUS 1

You mean sister. You ain't got no balls to me yo!

FETUS 2 tries hard to bend over and check its lower body.

FETUS 2

Really? So dark here. I see nothing.

FETUS 1

Exactly.

WOMAN opens an envelope and reads the letter.

WOMAN

"Hi Liz,
I hope you are well..."

She tears the letter up.

FETUS 1

I can't wait to get out and get rid of you.

FETUS 2

Why do you always want to get out? Don't you like it here?
Warm, soft, and there is always water and food. And we don't
need to move a finger.

FETUS 1

Don't make me laugh. Do you even have fingers?

FETUS 2 isn't sure. It tries to figure out but fails.

FETUS 2
I'm not sure... Does that mean we are fish? Or maggots... Just born and get flushed down the toilet the next minute.

FETUS 1
Oh my god. Stop making me nervous. I think I deserve to be a mammal at least.

FETUS 2
I wouldn't mind being a pony. Galloping on the grassland and playing with mud in the pond. Or a kitty cat. Chasing a ball of yarn must be fun.

FETUS 1
Or a tiger. With the power of tearing up everything. Or an elephant! The earth would be shaking when I walked or took a dump.

FETUS 2
Or an alligator! Resting under the sun but can attack like a strike of lightning and eat the prey with a single bite!

FETUS 1
But none of those can compare to:

FETUS 2
The pleasure of being a human!

FETUS 1
A human being!

WOMAN opens another envelope and reads the letter.

WOMAN

"Hi Liz,

Hope you are well.

Don't mean to disrupt your life again. Just want you to know. I got beaten up yesterday. Here murderers are mad dogs. Everyone leaves them alone. And economic criminals are the most respected. People think they've got a brain compared to the rest. But rapists are seen as the most disgusting. Everyone can spit on you. They broke my nose. I lay on the floor and thought, I probably deserve this. Not that I think they're any better than me, but I think I deserve it. Hope that would make you feel better. "

WOMAN tears up the letter and spits on it.

FETUS 1

Imagine being a human!

FETUS 2

There are so many things we can do!

WOMAN opens new envelopes, one after another, and tears them up.

FETUS 1

We can speak and write, and other people will understand us.

FETUS 2

And... and we can enjoy music and even play some ourselves!

FETUS 1

Music! What is that like?

FETUS 2

I don't know. Must be amazing!

FETUS 1

And we can eat cooked meals. And think of deep things like...
like... philosophy and physics and politics...

FETUS 2

Or simply another human being.

FETUS 1

Another human being. Definitely not you. Who will I think of...
Hmm... Must be someone marvelous and special. Can't wait to
see what that human looks like!

FETUS 2

And we will have families. In a big house! It must be wonderful to
have a family.

FETUS 1

I think, our father is a king and our mother is a queen. They are
the most beautiful and gentle parents in the world.

FETUS 2

And they love each other very much. *(Pause)* What does "love"
feel like?

FETUS 1

Like when every time there is food coming? How would I know? I
never loved.

FETUS 2

But you are going to! We are going to *loooooove*.

WOMAN reads another letter.

WOMAN

"I can't help thinking what it would be like otherwise and
wondering how I ended up here. What would I be doing on a

Sunday morning like this? How would it feel walking freely under the sun, stopping by a pizza shop with friends, and knowing no one hates my guts? Liz, I hope you will recover. You are such a bright girl. I hope you can finish college and forget what happened and have a wonderful life. I'm sorry for what I did. I hope we both could have another chance..."

> *She tears up the letter furiously. She hits her belly hard.*

FETUS 2

Ahhh! Awww! Aw! Aw!

FETUS 1

Aw! Aw! What's going on? Aw!! AAAAH!

FETUS 2

I don't know! ARRRGH! Are we dying?

FETUS 1

No way! I haven't even lived!

> *TWO FETUSES cry. WOMAN stops. She cries too.*

FETUS 2

I'm so scared.

FETUS 1

God please please please! I don't mind if I'm a maggot anymore as long as you let me live and take a look at the world outside.

FETUS 2

It stopped. We survived!

> *They hug each other.*

111

> ### FETUS 1

I'm hungry again.

> ### FETUS 2

Me too.

> *WOMAN eats more cheese puffs and drinks*
> *water and eats more and eats any food she can*
> *find.*

> ### FETUS 1

So warm here.

> ### FETUS 2

So soft.

> ### FETUS 1

Is this the feeling of love? I think there must be someone loving us right now.

> ### FETUS 2

Our parents!

> ### FETUS 1

Who are king and queen!

> *WOMAN suddenly feels a great pain.*

> ### FETUS 2

Ah...wait...

> ### FETUS 1

Stop doing that. Stand still.

> *WOMAN is in labor.*

It's not me... Hold my hand! Ahhh! Don't let me go!

FETUS 1

Stop it! Stop it you idiot! Where are you going? Hey! Hey! I've got you! I've got you! Hey...! Where did you go? Where are you idiot? Hey! Hey!

> *FETUS 2 disappears. FETUS 1 is alone and scared.*

FETUS 1

Where did you go? Don't leave me alone here...

> *Blackout.*

> *Lights up. FETUS 1 isn't on stage either. Only the WOMAN holding two babies and singing a lullaby gently.*

The postcard that inspired Wombmates.

SEVEN CHINESE BROTHERS

SEVEN CHINESE BROTHERS was produced by Youngblood at Ensemble Studio Theatre in New York City as part of "Asking for Trouble," a festival of short plays inspired by randomly-chosen elements, October 8-12, 2013. It was directed by Colleen Sullivan. The cast was as follows:

OA/TA THE GANG LEADER	Michael Tisdale
HOTSHOT THE GANGSTER	Seth Kirschner
PETE THE TATTOO MASTER	Bob Jaffe
BABY's VOICE	Bob Jaffe

The play was inspired by the title, the three wonderful actors, and an American Chinese restaurant delivery menu for a prop, which were all assigned to the playwright by lottery.

SCENE ONE

*PETE is relaxing and enjoying a cigarette in his
tattoo shop.*

HOTSHOT enters. He has only one arm.

HOTSHOT

Put out the cigarette.

PETE

What?
Hey man, what happened to your arm?!

HOTSHOT

Put out the cigarette NOW!

PETE

What's wrong with you, man?

*HOTSHOT takes out a gun and shoots in the
air.*

PETE

Fuck! Alright. Alright!

PETE puts out the cigarette.

HOTSHOT respectfully waits by the door.

HOTSHOT

Sir, all clear.

*OA enters very, very slowly with a baby
stroller. He waves a hand to clear the air around
the baby, as he can still smell the cigarette.*

117

HOTSHOT finds a chair and offers it to OA to sit.

OA

So you are the one tattooed my boys?

HOTSHOT

Yes sir. It was totally him!

OA

Oh, was I talking to you?

HOTSHOT

Sorry sir!

PETE

Yes... Yes sir. Wha... what's wrong?

OA

Please call me OA. Do you know what OA stands for?

PETE

Osteoarthritis?

HOTSHOT

Shut up! Shut up! Shut up!

OA

Yes, that too, but in my case, OA stands for "one arm."

PETE

But you have two arms. He is the one lost the arm... OH.

OA

I see you got the point. So don't piss me off, ok? Now, tell me who gave you the right to tattoo Chinese on all of my boys.

PETE

They... they said they wanted something cool.

OA

So you tattooed them with Chinese? Who the fuck you think we are? Are we still Italian Mafia or Fuk Ching Gang? This is no dignity!

> *OA takes out a big machete from under the baby stroller. The baby cries.*
>
> *OA puts down the machete and carefully picks up the baby. But it cries harder.*

OA

Shh... Shh... I'm sorry. I'm sorry. Shhh... *(To Pete)* You, come here. So you speak Chinese? Say something to my son.

PETE

(Takes a look at the baby)

This is your son?! He is not your son.

HOTSHOT

What do you know! OA bought him from China, ok?

OA

I didn't "bought" Bibi! I adopted him. He is my son! It hurts when you say things like that!

HOTSHOT and PETE

I'm sorry.

OA

Now say some Chinese to my son to calm him down.

PETE

I...

OA

Tell Bibi I love him. And I will be the best father. Tell him.

PETE

Uh... Ok...
Ching ching chang chang ching ching chang.

Baby stops crying for a beat.

OA

Good job!

*Baby cries again. OA hands the baby over to
HOTSHOT. Baby stops crying.*

OA

Damn.

HOTSHOT

Bibi likes me.

OA
(To Pete)

What did you tattoo on him?

HOTSHOT

"Brave heart"!

OA
(To Pete)

There is a way I can forgive you. Do you know what's "gentle
love" in Chinese?

                    PETE
Yeah.

                    OA
Tell me.

                    PETE
Ching Chang.

                    OA
Sounds good. Give me that tattoo for free.

                    PETE
No way, man!

                    OA
Fifty percent off.

                    PETE
No!

            OA goes to get the machete.

                    PETE
Fine! Ten percent off.

                    OA
Forty percent.

                    PETE
Twenty percent... Ok! Ok! Thirty percent off.

                    OA
Deal.

                    121

PETE plays Chinese traditional music on his iPod.

PETE

Please sit down. Close your eyes. Take a deep breath. Relax your muscles. And free your mind. Your soul is departing. It's traveling across time and space. You are flying through so many doors made with bright light. Two thousand years pass by. Finally, you hear soft music playing somewhere. You fly towards the sound, and land in front of a beautiful Chinese palace, that's where one of the oldest nations started and where one of the oldest languages was created. You can smell lotus flowers in the air. These are the lotus blossoming two thousand years ago. Your heart is filled with joy. Because you and this great ancient culture are becoming one.

OA bursts into tears. PETE starts to tattoo OA. Lights down.

Blackout.

SCENE TWO

A half-hour later.

Lights up.

PETE is alone in his shop smoking a cigarette. HOTSHOT rushes in with no arms. Blood on him.

HOTSHOT

Put out the cigarette!

PETE

Hey man, back so soon? What happened to your other arm?!

HOTSHOT

I said put out the cigarette!

PETE

Or what?

Silence.

OA enters with a machete in hand and a baby stroller. Blood on him too.

OA

Put out the cigarette.

PETE puts out the cigarette.

PETE

Hey, OA. What brings you guys back? What happened to his other arm?

OA

I chopped it off. Call me TA now. Two Arms. Hey, can you please explain this to me?

TA hands PETE a Chinese restaurant delivery menu.

TA

We were just ordering food next door. And somehow these characters look very similar to the ones on my arm.

PETE

No way. You must be kidding, man.

                              TA

You don't think so? Look closer. "Lunch special" — EXACTLY
THE SAME. And this—

                    *TA takes out a chopped off arm under the
                    stroller.*

                              TA

This says— *(He searches and compares on the menu for a while)*
"General Tso's Chicken." Yeah. "General Tso's Chicken." Same
pattern.

                          HOTSHOT

I fucking hate you, man! Why are you doing this to us!?

                            PETE

I don't know Chinese.

                          HOTSHOT

WHAT? You told us you learned Chinese, and Kongfu, and
Tattoo from a master in Shaolin.

                            PETE

I've never been to China.

                          HOTSHOT

At least you could pick some nice words from Google Translate!
Why did you have to choose from a menu!!!

                            PETE

The restaurant gives me a five-percent discount if I help them
with advertising.

                              TA

How many of my men have got tattoos from him?

HOTSHOT

I don't know. Like... six... seven...?

TA
(To Pete)
What did you put on the others?

PETE

I don't remember, man. One was beef broccoli I think. Another was... chop suey?

HOTSHOT

Cue Ball got the chop suey! I remember it looks like these characters. Oh man. He was so proud of it. Showing it around... You will break his heart.

PETE

Sorry man...

TA

Wait a second! Chop Suey — eleven dollars. Beef Broccoli — ten dollars. General Tso's Chicken — ten dollars. Lunch Special — five dollars. Why they got something like way more expensive than mine? Who is the boss?

HOTSHOT

Five dollars is not even enough for free delivery. It's a ten-dollar minimum, sir.

TA

Shut the fuck up! *(To Pete)* Which arm do you prefer?

PETE

Please... I'm so sorry.

                              TA

You shouldn't have messed with me.

                             PETE

I'm so sorry!

                              TA

Choose an arm.

                    The baby cries.

                              TA

Hotshot, go hold the baby.

                           HOTSHOT

I can't, sir.

          TA picks up the baby. The baby still cries.

                              TA

Shhhh... Bibi don't cry. *(To Pete)* Choose an arm.

                             PETE

Hey you know what! I can add an egg roll!

                   TA looks at the menu.

                   Baby keeps crying.

                              TA

Egg roll is two dollars. Choose an arm.

                             PETE

And a wonton soup! A wonton soup!

                   TA looks at the menu.

Baby cries harder.

TA

Wonton soup is only two dollars. Stop fooling me.

PETE

Rice! And rice. In total, ten dollars! It's a decent meal!

> *Baby cries harder and harder and suddenly — all is silent.*

> *Lights down. Only a spotlight on the baby.*

BABY

(A mature male voice)

My name is Ying Zheng. I'm the first emperor of China.

I was born in a war in 259 B.C. and inherited the throne of Qin from my father when I was only thirteen. By the age of thirty-nine, I had defeated all my enemies and conquered the six kingdoms. I was the king of the kings, the ruler of the universe. To strengthen the power of center, I standardized the units of measurements, such as weights and measures, the currency… Most importantly, I unified the Chinese script. I abolished the scripts of all the conquered regions and formed one language. So that everyone on earth could understand my orders. But sadly, there were still barbarians who couldn't be civilized by our great culture. To prevent them from encroaching on the frontiers, I ordered the construction of an immense defensive wall. Thousands of men died from building the Great Wall. The rest who didn't want to build it, I killed them. But myself, I feared death more than any of them. So I sent out teams everywhere to seek the elixir of life for me. And after being scammed countless times, I finally found the real medicine for immortality. I died when I was forty-nine, but I knew I would come back one day.

127

But I don't recognize this world around me. I don't understand this language. And they don't look like my people. Are they the barbarians? My Great Wall didn't work? My offspring failed me. Let me get up! Let me get up! The world has fallen apart. I shall conquer it again. Oh, my legs are so weak. My arms are so short. Hear me out! Hear me out! Your emperor has returned.

Spotlight off. The whole stage lights up again.

TA

Bibi stopped crying! Bibi stopped crying! For the first time, he stopped crying when I hold him! He must like my tattoo!

HOTSHOT

Shhh! Did you hear that?

PETE

What?

TA

Shh… Listen.

They listen closer.

TA

Oh my god. I think, I think Bibi just said "dad." OH MY GOD!

They hug one another.

End of play.

THE OFFENDED AUDIENCE

THE OFFENDED AUDIENCE was produced by Equally Represented Arts at the Chapel in St. Louis, April 22-May 8, 2015, as part of *R+J: A Telephone Play or Don't Drink the Milk*. It was directed by Lucy Cashion, lighting design by Erik Kuhn, costumes design by Meredith LaBounty, stage management by Gabe Taylor, and hair & make-up by Brooklynn Mcdade and Bernadette Marty. The cast was as follows:

ACTOR	Will Bonfiglio
AUDIENCE 1	Cara Barresi
AUDIENCE 2	Mitch Eagles
AUDIENCE 3	Rachel Tibbetts

ACTOR

So, we've reached a consensus. Weighing all the options—We are going to offend you, the audience.

Audience 1, 2, and 3 clap.

ACTOR

Thank you. Thank you. Yeah. That's what we are going to do.

AUDIENCE 1

That's bold.

AUDIENCE 3

That's what I call living theater!

AUDIENCE 2

I wonder if they are going to really offend us or just act like offending us.

ACTOR

Oh it's going to be real. You WILL BE offended.

AUDIENCE 2

Just to make sure. A lot of plays claim to be offensive these days, but end up being amusing, touching, boring, frightening or sexually arousing. You probably think that's because I'm a nice person so I'm not easily offended. No.

AUDIENCE 1

None of us are nice people. If you are nice, you don't come to theater. You go to church.

AUDIENCE 3

Or heaven.

ACTOR

Tell me. What can I do to offend you?

AUDIENCE 2

It's actually not that hard. Just ask me anything I don't know in front of a large group of people, and that would bring back the darkest memory in my life. In school, all I wanted was to hide in the dark of the back row and be invisible. I tried my best to avoid eye contact with teachers, but still, the teachers always called me up. And I would just freeze there, like an idiot, having no idea what to say. Everyone was looking. That became the scar I've carried my whole life.

ACTOR

Ok. Got it. "Exposing the audience's ignorance." *(To Audience 1)* How about you?

AUDIENCE 1

Once I was really offended in a Knicks game. I was there with my boyfriend at that time. We just had a fight. And the next thing you know, we were on the kiss cam. Neither of us moved. The camera waited and waited. And the crowd wouldn't leave us alone. They whistled and laughed. Oh god. We broke up right after the game.

AUIDENCE 3

Did you wish you kissed?

AUDIENCE 1

No, but I knew we would after an hour, or a day, or a week, and we would be fine. It wasn't the first time we fought. We would still be together and probably married if it weren't that fucking camera. That fucking camera pointed a gun on our heads right at that spot.

AUDIENCE 3

I would be offended if you proposed to me, now.

AUDIENCE 3 directs ACTOR. ACTOR
follows whatever she says.

AUDIENCE 3

We are just chatting like everyone else, and boom! Out of nowhere
my whole family, your whole family, my boss, my high school
friends, my childhood neighbors… all pop up. And you're down
on one knee, and hand me a little box. You tell me that my sister
helped you pick the ring. A song plays in the background. It's the
one we danced to on our first date.

A romantic/celebratory song plays. The
AUDIENCE cheer.

AUDIENCE 3

You look into my eyes and say,

ACTOR

You are the love of my life. Will you marry me?

AUDIENCE 1

Yes! Yes! Marry him!

AUDIENCE 2

Good luck buddy!

The AUDIENCE cheer more.

AUDIENCE 1
(Weeping)

This is so romantic.

ACTOR

Will you marry me?

                    AUDIENCE 3

And that would offend me very much. That would make me sick
to my stomach.

                    AUDIENCE 2

Wait. That's how *I* proposed to you.

                    AUDIENCE 3

Yeah.

                    AUDIENCE 2

And you said yes!

                    AUDIENCE 3

Actually I was going to break up with you that night, but what
else could I say? No? In a situation like that?

                    AUDIENCE 2

What? You didn't want to marry me?

                    AUDIENCE 3
                     (Quietly)

No.

                     ACTOR

Got it. "Emotional hijacking."

                    AUDIENCE 2

Do you love me?

                    AUDIENCE 3

Not really.

                    AUDIENCE 2

It's been ten years and you never told me?

AUDIENCE 3

What do you want now? Divorce me in public?

AUDIENCE 1

I get offended when other audience members are talking during the show. Actors talking is good. Actors and audience talking to each other is good. It's called interaction. Only the audience talking? Uh-uh. That's offensive. It's not theater. It's pure noise in a theatrical space, which should be called intermission.

AUDIENCE 2

A play offends me once it goes on longer than two hours.

AUDIENCE 3

No play deserves more than ninety minutes of my life.

AUDIENCE 1

A play offends me if I can't figure out what it's about after five minutes. (Checks her watch) It's been thirty minutes and I still don't know what this play is about. I'm offended.

AUDIENCE 2

A play offends me if other audience members laugh so hard and I don't.

AUDIENCE 3

A play offends me when it makes me cry and realize I'm crying at the same time.

AUDIENCE 1

A play offends me when it asks personal questions, such as

ACTOR

(To a real audience member)

When was the last time you had sex?

ZHU YI

AUDIENCE 1
(To a real audience member)
What's your favorite position?

AUDIENCE 2
(To a real audience member)
Have you ever cheated on your partner?

AUDIENCE 3
(To a real audience member)
How old are you?

ACTOR
(To a real audience member)
How much money do you make?

AUDIENCE 1
(To a real audience member)
Tell me a story about your childhood,

AUDIENCE 2
(To a real audience member)
When you wanted to kill yourself.

AUDIENCE 3
(To a real audience member)
When you wished you were another person.

ACTOR
(To a real audience member)
When you hurt someone and regretted it.

AUDIENCE 1
(To a real audience member)
Tell me about your father.

AUDIENCE 2
(To a real audience member)
Tell me about your ex.

AUDIENCE 3
(To a real audience member)
In front of your date.

ACTOR
(To a real audience member)
In front of your mother in law.

AUDIENCE 1
(To the real audience)
Who farted?

AUDIENCE 2
(To a real audience member)
Was that you?

AUDIENCE 3
(To a real audience member)
You?

ACTOR
(To a real audience member)
I think it's her/him. You can still smell it around this area.

AUDIENCE 1
Whoever farted, please leave. I mean it.

Silence.

ACTOR stares at the one real audience member, threatening. Finally he lets it go.

137

ACTOR

No. It's not her/him.

Dear audience, I have a good news. There will be a dance party in the end of the show. You will be invited, or more accurately, forced to join the stage in your extra-large T-shirt, sweatpants and flipflops, and you will interact with our cast, who are professionally trained dancers with amazing body shapes and stage makeup. Dance! Dance like no one is watching, except everyone is watching! Your mama is watching. Your grandma is watching. Your auntie Ruth and her teenage daughter are watching.

> *Night club music starts. AUDIENCE 1,2, and 3 lead the dance.*

AUDIENCE 1

Come on baby! Put your hands up! Put your hands up! Shake your butt, shake it, shake it, shake your butt!

AUDIENCE 2

Are you having fun? Let's say—HEYYYY!

AUDIENCE 1,2, 3 and ACTOR

HEYYYYY!

AUDIENCE 2

Let's say—YEAAAAH!

AUDIENCE 1,2, 3 and ACTOR

YEAAAAH!

AUDIENCE 1

Dance! Dance like a motherfucker! Dance! Dance like you've been drinking all night except you are completely sober.

138

ACTOR

You missed a lot of beats, but it's okay. You are not the only one looking stupid!

AUDIENCE 1

Just pretend you are having a nice time.

AUDIENCE 2

Just pretend you are cool.

AUDIENCE 3

Pretend you fit into society perfectly.

Music stops.

ACTOR

That's what we gonna do in the end of the show. Everybody will have a chance to participate. And after the group dance, we will choose one of you to give a solo dance. Isn't it amazing? So please keep that in mind and prepare yourself.

AUDIENCE 1

And if you dare to leave early, we will know. The audience area is like a desert. Once you stand up, you are completely exposed.

AUDIENCE 2

You will be on your own, no longer protected by the rules. You are not part of the audience and you are not part of the cast. Who are you? You are a ghost intruding into a dream.

ACTOR

And that could be very dangerous.

AUDIENCE 3

Once I was late to a show.

AUDIENCE 2

First I had to walk pass the entire front row.

AUDIENCE 1

And my seat was deep inside the second row.

AUDIENCE 3

So the entire second row had to stand up to let me pass.

AUDIENCE 2

Half of them were old people. Took forever to get up and sit down.

AUDIENCE 1

When I finally reached my seat. My phone rang.

Sound of iPhone ringtone goes on and on.

AUDIENCE 3

Oh god.

AUDIENCE 2

And I couldn't find it in my bag.

AUDIENCE 1

The actor was in the middle of a monologue—a suicide note.

ACTOR	AUDIENCE 3
Of Man's first disobedience, and the fruit	Argh!
Of that forbidden tree whose mortal taste	*AUDIENCE 3 sighs. Phone keeps ringing.*
Brought death into the World, and all our woe,	AUDIENCE 2
With loss of Eden, till one	God.

140

greater Man
Restore us, and regain the
blissful seat,
Sing, Heavenly Muse, that, on
the secret top
Of Oreb, or of Sinai, didst
inspire
That shepherd who first
taught the chosen seed
In the beginning how the
heavens and earth
Rose out of Chaos: or, if Sion
hill
Delight thee more, and Siloa's
brook that flowed
Fast by the oracle of God, I
thence
Invoke thy aid to my
adventurous song,
That with no middle flight
intends to soar...

*The ACTOR doesn't have
to finish all these lines. He
can stop whenever the
AUDIENCE's lines finish.*

*The three AUDIENCE make
all kinds of small sounds to
protest. And they make it
louder and louder as the
ringtone goes on and on, and
they get angrier and angrier.*

AUDIENCE 1
(Shouts)
Turn it off!

AUDIENCE 3
Show some respect!

AUDIENCE 2
What a bitch!

AUDIENCE 1
People are trying to see a show
here!

AUDIENCE 3
Throw her out!

AUDIENCE 2
Perfect. Now I can't hear
anything.

AUDIENCE 1
All her fault. Burn that witch!

AUDIENCE 1
(Shouts)
Burn that witch!

                                    AUDIENCE 1, 2, 3 and ACTOR
                                        (Shouting in rhythm)
                                    Burn that witch! Burn that
                                    witch! Burn that witch!

                        AUDIENCE 3
All of sudden, the ringtone stopped. A voice came from the other
side of the phone.

                            VOICE
Hello?

                        AUDIENCE 3
Hello?

                            VOICE
I'm God. I don't like what I see. It's been too long, too tedious.
And you asked me a lot of questions I couldn't answer. A lot of
personal questions. And no. I don't love you. Stop telling
everyone I do. I am offended. I don't like your performance. It's
bad acting. You don't know your characters. You only care about
whether you are good-looking. I'm leaving. Where is the casting
director? I'm gonna give him a call tonight and tell him to cast my
son.

                        AUDIENCE 2
And he hung up.

                        AUDIENCE 1
That was a joke, right?

                        AUDIENCE 3
No.

AUDIENCE 1

That... was that really... him?

AUDIENCE 3

Yes.

ACTOR

And we were frightened.

AUDIENCE 1

I didn't mean to...

AUDIENCE 2

Me neither.

ACTOR

Can you call him back?

AUDIENCE 3

I don't know how.

AUDIENCE 1

He really left?

They look around and look up.

They search in the audience.

AUDIENCE 2
(To the real audience)

Hello?

ACTOR
(To the real audience)

What I said about the dance in the end, it's not true. I made it up.
There won't be any dance. We will not force you or even suggest

143

you to join the stage. You are safe. You are safe. We guarantee your safety.

                    AUDIENCE 1

Oh.

                    AUDIENCE 2

Good to know. That's been troubling me.

                    ACTOR

Please don't leave us alone here. Please. You don't have to answer any questions. Just watch us from your seat. We will be good. I promise. I've already known better about my character. I'm figuring him out. Are you still there?

                    Silence.

                    AUDIENCE 3

What now?

                    AUDIENCE 1

You promised to offend us.

                    ACTOR

I thought I wouldn't care, but it actually hurts when I know someone doesn't like what I do.

                    AUDIENCE 3

What should we do now?

                    AUDIENCE 2

What should we do now?

                    Blackout.

                    End of play.

ABOUT THE AUTHOR

ZHU YI is a New York-based playwright and screenwriter, born and raised in China. She received her MFA in playwriting from Columbia University. She is a 2012-2013 Emerging Artist Fellow at New York Theatre Workshop, a Youngblood Writer at Ensemble Studio Theatre, a member of Dramatists Guild of America, a member of Chinese Pioneering Filmmakers Association, and an adjunct lecturer at Nanjing University, China. www.zoezhu.com.

Stage plays: *I Am a Moon* (FringeNYC; Edinburgh Fringe, United Kingdom; Mu Ma Theater, China; 3LD Art and Technology Center, New York City; Global Voices: Spring Staged Readings, Theater Emory, Atlanta, Georgia), *How Time Flies* (National Theatre of China; Beijing Capital Theatre, China; National tour in China), *Holy Crab!* (Unfiltered Festival, Ensemble Studio Theatre, New York City), *The Offended Audience* (*R+J: A Telephone Play* , the Chapel, Saint Louis, Missouri), *Long Life* (Shanghai Dramatic Arts Center, China), *Long Distance Affair* (Bienal Arte Joven Buenos Aires, Argentina; Edinburgh Fringe, United Kingdom), *Evolutionism* (Beijing Fringe, China; National Avant-Grade Theater, China; Manhattan Repertory Theater, New York City), *Lifetime Fairytale* (Riverside Theatre, New York City).

Films: *Scrape* (Taiwan International Documentary Film Festival; Alcances Film Festival, Spain; Beijing Independent Film Festival), *Apolitical Romance* (Best Feature Nomination at Taipei Film Festival; Buenos Aires International Independent Film Festival; New York Asian Film Festival; World Film Festival of Bangkok; Hawaii International Film Festival; Udine Far East Film Festival, Italy; Taipei Golden Horse Film Festival).

Made in the USA
Middletown, DE
09 October 2015